Neil Forsyth is an author and television writer. A fellow Dundonian and friend to Bob Servant for over two decades he has previously assisted Servant on three books, *Delete This At Your Peril – The Bob Servant Emails*, *Bob Servant – Hero of Dundee* and *Why Me? – The Very Important Emails of Bob Servant*. He also did what he could to help Servant on the BBC Radio 4 series *The Bob Servant Emails* and the BBC TV comedy *Bob Servant*. Forsyth is the author of *Other People's Money*, the biography of fraudster Elliot Castro, and the novels *Let Them Come Through* and *San Carlos*. He writes for television in the UK and the USA. In 2012, he memorably came third in the *Dundee Evening Telegraph*'s Spirit of Dundee competition, losing to television presenter Lorraine Kelly and the Verdant Works Jute Museum.

Previous Praise

'A former cheeseburger magnate and semi-retired window cleaner, Bob is a delightfully deranged but likeable rogue. A living, breathing creation of comic genius...Today, Broughty Ferry. Tomorrow, the world?' *Bookbag*

'*Bob Servant* is a very, very funny book. You will piss yourself and then quote sections of this book repeatedly within your circle of friends.' *Irvine Welsh*

'Bob Servant has attained national treasure status' *Scotsman*

★ 'Didn't do it for me, a bit lazy...I just didn't connect with Bob as a person.' *M. Thomas, Amazon.co.uk*

'I have worked with Peter Cook and Spike Milligan. Bob Servant is in a class of his own' *Barry Fantoni, Private Eye*

'This is one of the funniest books ever compiled...the work of a comedy genius.' *Skinny*

'Neil Forsyth is one of the finest comic writers working today' *Scotland on Sunday*

★★ 'Quite frankly, Bob was an imbecile. If he actually had a brain the book might not have seemed so poor. But alas, no brain for Bob.'
Amelia, GoodReads.com

'Genuinely hilarious...had me crying with laughter. Bob Servant is a modern Scottish comedy classic, and entirely deserves his hero status.'
Press & Journal

'Cracklingly funny, a laugh on every page.' *Herald*

'Hurrah for *Bob Servant*! Read it in private as it will make you laugh out loud.' *Book Magazine*

★ 'A primary schoolboy could do better. As a proud Dundonian I was not at all enamoured. There is no need to trivialize the wonderful humour of this great city' *E. B. R., Amazon.co.uk*

'*Bob Servant Independent* was the wonderful surprise of the week. A total joy from start to finish – original, sharp, superbly acted and gloriously funny. A little gem of a comedy, don't miss it.' *The Times*

'Likeable and amusing...Cox is clearly having a whale of a time and his relish is infectious. An idiotic, roaring blow-hard, Servant is a welcome addition to our rich history of sitcom monsters. He may even do for Dundee what Alan Partridge did for Norwich.' *Scotsman*

'I found myself simultaneously thinking that it was all getting a bit silly and laughing at it at the same time. There's something joyfully inventive about Bob's foolishness too, a sideways skitter that keeps throwing up lines you couldn't quite have predicted. Hard to categorise, but the fact that it is is one of its pleasures.' *Independent*

'A puffed-up, overbearing, delusional twat...the worst and most pompous pub bore you can possibly imagine...extreme vanity...quite bizarre.'
New Statesman

ASK BOB

Your Guide To
A Wonderful Life

BOB
SERVANT

Edited by
Neil Forsyth

For Rhiannon, my skirt, with love

Contents

: Introduction :
by Neil Forsyth

When Bob contacted me and demanded I edit another of his books, my reaction was one of overriding fear. I've known Bob for 25 years and it has been mentally expensive. He lives a life that is driven by whimsy and teeters on the edge of lunacy. Spending too long in his force field can do awful things to you. Just look at his lifelong sidekick, Frank, a desperately troubled man who once turned to me and whispered 'Help me' while Bob was sleeping beside us on a bus.

After a career as a window cleaner and a cheeseburger-van operator of some repute, Bob became an unlikely author and star of a Radio 4 series and BBC TV documentary. Now, Bob told me, he was writing a new book for Random House. 'Which is funny,' he added, his voice already trembling with anticipation of the joke, 'because I often wake up at a random house.' He laughed for – and if anything I'm rounding down – three minutes.

For nearly a decade, Bob has been answering people's problems. *Ask Bob* began as an email newsletter that went to a handful of associates in Dundee, the hometown of Bob and myself. Soon, the newsletter had spread to a thousand email addresses around the world. When the books, the radio and the TV show arrived, it grew even larger. For this book, Bob has diligently addressed a huge new batch of letters.

Once again I travelled home to Broughty Ferry, Dundee, and spent long, troubling hours wading through Bob's files. The result is a journey into the opinions, life and unique mind of Bob Servant. As always, I have left Bob's words untouched. Here and there I have offered supporting documentation from Bob's records, and the occasional footnote. Dealing with Bob was awful.[1] I have included some sample text exchanges in a cheap attempt to gain your sympathy for my plight.

Of all the reviews that Bob and I have had for the books, radio and TV shows, my favourite came from a Christian youth lifestyle magazine. 'These are the writings,' read the review, 'of a clearly deranged mind.' That came from someone who had spent perhaps an hour in Bob's company.

I have spent a lifetime.

Help me.

---

1   See the Acknowledgements section, where I deal with Bob and it's awful.

Enquiries at the burger van or in person at Stewpot's Bar, Broughty Ferry, after 6pm.
Not Bank Holidays (brings out the nutters).

A big 'Hello' from Bob Servant!

Another book. Number four! Forgot the trilogy, now it's a ~~qaud qud quado~~ there's four of them!

Of all the many, many glories I have enjoyed in my life, nothing has given me more pleasure than dealing with you, the happy punters through all those years of the much-admired Ask Bob. So many of you, from all over the world, have sent me your very worst problems, and I have heroically solved every single one.

When I finally shuffle off to the big disco in the sky, folk will say all sorts about me. They'll talk about me being a good man to have about the place, how I pretty much had the lot, and they'll talk at (almost) embarrassing length about my sexual energy. They'll say I left the punters howling with pleasure, that I sold Broughty Ferry to the world, and that I took on the boo boys and came out with my head held right up in the clouds.

But forget all that. Because of Ask Bob, they'll say something else. They'll say, 'And do you know what else Bob Servant did? He helped.'

I did. I helped. And I was absolutely delighted to do so.

Your Servant,

Bob Servant

What a piece of work is a man! How noble in reason, how infinite in faculty, in form and moving how express and admirable, in action how like an angel, in apprehension how like a god! The beauty of the world, the paragon of animals!
William Shakespeare (1564–1616)

The creations of a great writer are little more than the moods and passions of his own heart, given surnames and Christian names, and sent to walk the earth.
W. B. Yeats (1865–1939)

In 1983 I accidentally wore my jumper inside out to a bowling club disco in Carnoustie. Sometimes I wonder if I ever recovered.
Bob Servant (1945–)

Family

Bob,

My mother-in-law's perfume is extremely strong. I think it's some eighties concoction called 'Lust' or 'Hot Spice' or suchlike. What can I do?

'Overpowered', Brighton

When two skunks meet each other on a mountain path they spray each other down and continue on their way. In much the same way, you need to start wearing the same scent as your mother-in-law. Over time, you will become immune to the smell and diminish her power as a result. The only slight downside is that there is a fairly high chance your father-in-law will become sexually attracted to you. If this happens then you have to 'turn him off'. The easiest way is to find out which of your mother-in-law's dresses he finds the least attractive and wear it whenever in his company. That should cool his misplaced passions and allow you to retain every possible shred of dignity.

———

Dear Bob,

I'm receiving a decent amount of pelters from the wife about the household finances. She says that I think life is like a big game of

Monopoly but I've always thought it's more like KerPlunk. I think she should leave it to me but she's not really buying that approach. Who should run the money side of the family game, Bob?

Harry T, Belfast

I've seen a lot of good men brought down through 'dough debates' with their wives. My pal Tommy Peanuts got so sick of it that he put his family's finances in the hands of his cocker spaniel Biscuits. He'd write down all the family's bills and get Biscuits to pick out the most important ones using his paw. It was a fair compromise and, most importantly, a good laugh. These days Tommy does his own finances though, as they don't allow dogs in the hostel.

———————

Bob,

I'm fairly sure my brother's new wife stole a chicken wing from my plate at the weekend. I went off to check on the BBQ (I was having a bit of a Cumberland Crisis) and when I returned to the table I was one wing down and she was looking even more pleased with herself than usual. Not sure how best to handle it. I presume I should be alerting the authorities?

'A Wing and a Prayer', Warrington

Yes, one for the constabulary I'm afraid. To assist them with their enquiries, politely explain to her that she will be required to 'pass' into a bucket over the next few days with the rest of the family observing as witnesses. Yes, it will be an uncomfortable situation that will possibly lead to the breakdown of her fledgling marriage, but she's brought it all upon herself and given you literally no choice.

Bob,

My mother has been leering at my new boyfriend a bit, especially when she's been on the gin (so pretty much always). He's a good-looking man but it's getting ridiculous. How do I get her to wind it in?

'Uncomfortable', Glasgow

I feel for him because I've been wrestling with this one for years. Unfortunately, other than hit myself in the face with a hammer, there's not a huge amount I can do. I've just had to make small adjustments to my life to make things bearable. I try not to be in the vicinity of hen parties, for example, or my clothes will be shredded from my body within seconds and, if not physically stopped, they'll start nibbling at my flesh like eels. If I ever sit in public, I always make sure that I press my legs firmly together in case a woman is lurking nearby with binoculars and 'getting off' on the outline of my genitals through my corduroys. In the end I have had to wear a specially adapted outfit whenever I am in a crowded area, or it just gets out of hand (photo enclosed). I suggest your boyfriend adopts something similar for future family gatherings.

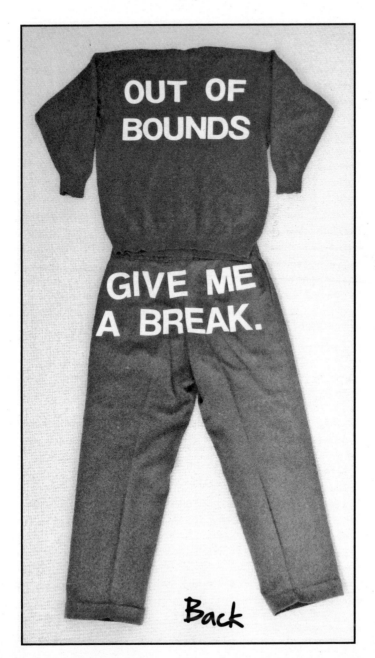

Hi Bob,

Our son has his first date at the weekend, the poor wee lad's a nervous wreck. We were hoping a man of your vast experience could advise us on how to support him at this challenging time?

Shuggy and Sara P, Inverness

You can support him by letting him have a wee 'run through'. Set up your kitchen as a fancy restaurant and invite your son in. For that all-important element of surprise it would be best if you, Shuggy, played the girl. Dress extremely provocatively and make various daring suggestions involving the black pepper. Sara, you will, inevitably, be playing the part of a lewd Italian waiter. Teach your son about the danger of male competition by flirting outrageously with Shuggy, having padded out your trousers to suggest your waiter character is in an excitable state. Your son will be put through a baptism of fire and will thank you for it, both now and in later years when he is happily married to a woman who may or may not resemble his father in drag.

Dear Bob,

Meeting the girlfriend's parents for the first time next weekend. How should I handle the dad?

'The Debutante', The Wirral

You need to find out if he's a good man and the easiest way to do that is to set a trap. When you're alone ask him if anyone has been giving him 'bother' because, if they have, you could arrange for that person's house to get 'torched'. Quickly move the conversation on and monitor him for the next few weeks. If he's at all nervous around you then he's clearly considering taking up your offer and, sadly, you'll have no choice but to report his criminal intentions to the constabulary.

Bob,

My brother's just become a dad and, I'm not sure how best to say this, his baby son has an adult-sized piece of 'equipment'. No-one else has mentioned it so I'm kind of in two minds of how best to play it. I mean, the thing must be a record breaker, surely the kid should be getting the attention and plaudits that he deserves?

'Proud Uncle', Derby

You're absolutely right, the kid is going to be a star, and the sooner those around him get used to it the better. In the next few months he's going to start picking up sponsorship deals from underwear firms, banana importers and drawbridge manufacturers. Then it's time to think about his autobiography, for which I humbly suggest the title *Willy the Kid*. To cut a long story short, he's about to be cast adrift into the shark-infested world of showbiz, he needs a manager, and you're the man for the job. Hand in your notice tomorrow. Simply tell your boss you're off to work full-time representing your nephew's penis, they'll almost definitely understand.

Bob,

Our family can never agree on what to watch on TV. The kid likes cartoons, my wife likes nature shows and I like stuff with nudity. And that's human nudity, Bob, so don't try to palm me off with the nature shows. How do we find a compromise?

'On the Box', Cheltenham

You've come to the right place. A few years ago, I created a TV character called Bob Sergeant. Bob Sergeant is a lovable rogue who shoots from the hip and doesn't give a flying shite for the rulebook. He's also, through no fault of his own, a helluva ladies man. I sent off a few episodes to the BBC and got a 'thanks but no thanks'. I'm not surprised, TV's a closed shop, it's all about who you know. Here's a wee bit of Bob Sergeant that should keep you and, more importantly, the family entertained.[2]

---

2   Bob generously allowed me access to his bewildering collection of Bob Sergeant scripts on the proviso that he retains all rights to TV, movies and 'branded duvet sets'.

THE BOB SERGEANT ADVENTURES
Episode 1 - "LADY MUCK"

FADE IN:

Int. office. Broughty ferry.

WE OPEN on the Office of Bob Sergeant, the Sexy Vet of
Broughty Ferry. Bob Sergeant is doing press ups on the
ground. He's done loads of them already and he's not
even that tired. He's done upwards of three hundred
press ups. Piece of piss.

A WOMAN ENTERS holding a RABBIT.

                    Bob
        Ah, you must be my ten o'clock.

He SPRINGS UP like a man who is like a cat.

                    Duchess
        I am. I'm a local Duchess and am
        having terrible problems with my
        rabbit. I think it might be dy-
        ing. Unfortunately.

                    Bob
        Well, you've come to the right
        place. I'm Bob Sergeant, the Sexy
        Vet of Broughty Ferry. Why don't
        you stick your rabbit down on my
        table and I'll give it the old
        once over.

Bob Sergeant's hair is slicked back with heavy lacquer.
It has very little give and that's A-OK because it looks
terrific.

                    DuchesS
        OK Dokey.

She PUTS DOWN THE RABBIT ON THE TABLE.

Bob Sergeant CARESSES THE RABBIT with his hands.

> Bob
> Duchess, take your worries and
> throw them into the bin because
> your rabbit is going to be abso-
> lutely fine. He's just twanged his
> paw. Let me pop it off and he'll
> be as right as rain.

> Duchess
> Oh thank Christ. Great news.

Bob Sergeant TAKES OFF HIS TUXEDO JACKET.

The Duchess goes GOGGLE-EYED looking at his BODY.

Bob begins SAWING OFF THE RABBIT'S PAW.

> Bob
> You know, in the wild, rabbits
> have a helluva time in the sack.
> That's where the 'ole saying
> comes from. "At it like rabbits".

Bob takes THE CIGAR out his mouth and taps the ash into
an ivory ashtray.

> Bob (CONT'D)
> Whaddya think about that?

Bob Sergeant often says American things like
"whaddya think".

The Duchess puts down her MARTINI GLASS.

                    Duchess
          Well, I gotta tell ya, that
          sounds pretty damn good from
          where I'm standing. I'm a local
          Duchess.

                    Bob
          In that case, what say we give
          those damm rabbits a run for
          their money?

                    DUCHESS
          Oooh yeah. Ooooh ooooh oooh
          yeah.

                    Bob
          OK.
                    Duchess
          Whatcha wanna do first?

Bob Sergeant presses a button and ALL HIS
CLOTHES FALL OFF.

close up:

ON THE RABBIT who ROLLS HIS EYES as if to say
"'Ere we go."

                    THE END

Dear Bob,

My husband's threatening to buy me a washer/dryer for Christmas. He says that's an acceptable gift after 17 years of marriage, but has promised to take your advice. Help.

'Hung Out To Dry', Northumberland

It's acceptable if he adds a suitably saucy touch. The obvious option would be for him to secrete himself naked within the machine and have a friend wrap it and push it under the tree. You'll assume he's gone missing, have an absolutely horrendous Christmas Eve and then enjoy the most wonderful twist on Christmas Day when he clambers out the machine as naked as the day he was born and suggests he takes you upstairs for a 'spin cycle'.

Hi Bob,

My boyfriend has started gardening and he's only 26. Please help me Bob, it's embarrassing, he's even got a shed.

Millie F, West Sussex

I'm afraid you'd better go and have a wee look in this shed. With luck, he's an alcoholic with an admirable love of privacy. But steel yourself, for I fear you may find several dozen jazz mags with famous people's faces crudely stuck onto the naked bodies. You need to ask yourself very, very carefully if entering that shed is something you want to do. Because, frankly, there's a high chance that there will also be some famous animals involved, such as Lassie and Zippy from Rainbow, and your brain would be fried forever by seeing some of the contortions your boyfriend may or may not have imagined for them.

Bob,

I met my fiancée's brother for the first time last night. Before we'd got our starters he'd shown me a photo of his car and told me how much he earns. I don't think I can ever spend another evening in his company. What's my next move?

'Greatly Concerned', Birmingham

Asking for the ring back and getting on with your life.

Dear Bob,

Got my Great Aunt Janet's funeral on Saturday. I've had to cancel playing five-a-side beforehand. I could have probably managed both but I would have been in my Adidas Sambas at the funeral and my wife said that would have been out of order. Anyway, I'm not sure how to play it at the funeral. All I remember about Janet is that she liked *Coronation Street* and wore the least convincing wig in Glasgow.

Yours respectfully

Bingo McKenzie, Glasgow

Despite spending the majority of her time pie-eyed on supermarket gin (an educated guess), your wife is right on this occasion. You need to hang up your Sambas and concentrate on giving Janet the send-off she deserves by attending the funeral in costume as filthy-minded *Coronation Street* legend Vera Duckworth. Use her 'Ooh ducky' catchphrase liberally upon arrival, and when the coffin begins its descent, call out, 'Ooh down she goes, and not for the first time' and let loose with one of Vera's much-loved cackles. It's the kind of bawdy observation that Janet would have loved and the other punters at the funeral will howl with laughter. Who knows, maybe inside the coffin Janet will have a last wee chuckle herself? Fingers crossed!

Bob,

That all sounds great. I'm sourcing the Vera outfit from charity shops. Can I ask for a couple more tips on the funeral? It's my first one apart from when we buried my uncle's cat Horatio, but that was a pretty informal affair. Do I tip the minister?

Bingo

Find enclosed my full Funeral Etiquette Guide. Please send £5.99 by return of post.[3]

---

3   Over the years, for unclear reasons, Bob has produced a wide range of etiquette guides. Distribution has been disappointing.

"Abide with Glee"
Bob Servant's
Guide to Funerals

1 Stand Out

If you want to be a big hit at the
funeral you need to swim against the
tide. Every man and his dog will be
muttering about the deceased being a
decent man or woman and how they only
killed their own and so on. Grab attention by saying you thought they were
"the absolute pits" and how you're only
there for the sandwiches. People will
admire your no-nonsense attitude and
give you an unholy amount of respect.

2. Seating
Often the deceased's family go out of their way to grab the best seats at a funeral. Get round their selfishness by taking your own deckchair and setting up shop at the front.

3. The Minister /Priest/Rabbi /Sheikh/Sensei
Get the main man/-woman on your side early doors by clapping above your head whenever they finish talking. When they finish their big speech, spray them all over with mid-range champagne. They'll feel like a famous Formula One driver and be forever in your debt.

Do NOT open until funeral

4. The Singing

When it comes to the hymns, there's always someone with a deep voice who arrogantly dominates proceedings. The easiest, and classiest, way round that is to take along a microphone and small portable speaker.

5. Cheering Up the Punters

People are sad at funerals and it's your job to cheer them up (no-one else is going to do it!). You can do some low level stuff outside the church — hand buzzers, 'finding' money behind ears - but it's once the service starts you can really get going. One way to turn the punters "tears into wine" is to wait until the coffin is on its way into the fire, throw a string of sausages on top of it and say you might as well "cook some bangers for the wake." It's a fun, visual joke that will have the punters clapping like seals.

Have a good one!

Bob,

Thanks for sending me such a professional-looking brochure. I particularly enjoyed the pictures, though that shouldn't for one moment suggest that I didn't also enjoy the words. I think I've got all the various bits of kit you suggest (I'm going to take some Tesco Finest 'Chipolata' sausages for an extra touch of class) but I was a wee bit surprised you didn't talk about what to wear. Surely I can't go to every funeral dressed as Vera Duckworth?

Bingo

Bingo, don't be ridiculous. For normal funerals just wear something appropriate. Traditionally, I wear the attached. It's dignified, chic and sends the relevant messages without being overly pushy.

Thanks Bob,

That looks perfect, I can't see how this could possibly go wrong.

Bingo

Neither can I, Bingo. Neither can I.

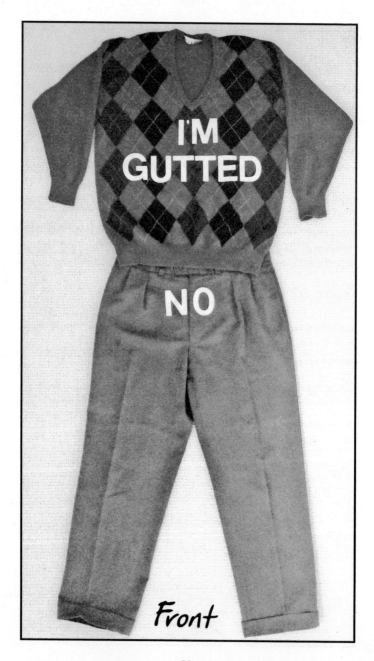

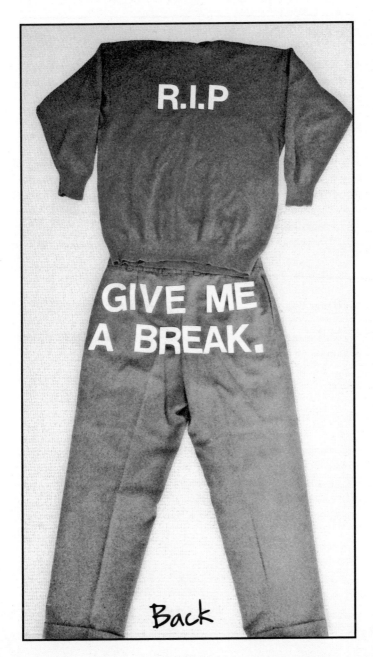

Dear Bob,

My daughter has started dating. As you can imagine it's a challenging time for me. Any advice on how to play the role of the protective father?

'Paternal Concerns', Shrewsbury

You need to keep an eye on them and I mean that literally. I'm talking, of course, about the art of camouflage. If they go bowling, you're in the next lane disguised as a schoolboy. If they're in the park, you're right behind them disguised as a bush. If they're at the cinema, you're disguised as an oh-so-tempting, leather-cushioned 'VIP' seat. With any luck, one of them will sit on you, giving you a bird's-eye view of proceedings. Stay vigilant.

Greetings Bob,

The kids want a dog, I'm not so sure. Please advise, Bob. We will, of course, go with your opinion.

Yours,

Bob C, Northchapel

Go for it, Bob. I grew up having a dog as one of my best pals, a German Shepherd called Jasper. Jasper was the absolute business – sporty, up for a laugh, and without any of the arrogance you'd traditionally expect from a German Shepherd. Unfortunately his owner moved to Fife in 1974 and Jasper and I lost touch. I wonder what he's doing now.

Bob,

What's an acceptable amount of money to lend a family member? My brother's out of work but my wife says I shouldn't give him money because he boozes like a madman.

'Brotherly Love', Teddington

The fact that he boozes like a madman is exactly the reason you should give him money. One of the many qualities of the heavy drinker is how many ideas they have. The great irony, of course, is that these ideas often strike at the very worst time – when the boozer is laying with great dignity on the pavement, or sleeping on a bus, or berating themselves in an alleyway. And even if they're capable of remembering the idea, they often lack the means to act on it, having spent their meagre resources on much needed refreshment, fast food and 'on the spot' fines from the constabulary. However, armed with your investment, your brother will put that money to use and you'll soon be rich beyond your wildest dreams. When you fan out your readies on your bed and invite your boo-boy wife to make love upon those tax-free notes, then I think her tune will change with immediate effect. It's a win-win-win.

Dear Bob,

Not a fan of my son's girlfriend, what can I do?

PS They're both five.

Andy W, Auckland

Visit the girl's parents and calmly explain that she's not a suitable companion for your son, you believe she is of questionable morals and wouldn't want to speculate how life is going to turn out for her. And then speculate, at length, using an array of detailed sketches of the girl all grown up and in various gritty pickles.

Bob,

The mother-in-law has started showing up every Friday night, and she's being an absolute gannet with the Chinese takeaway. I'm sent out to get it, I put the bags down and by the time I've got my jacket off she's wolfed down half the crispy duck. I'll not even start on the cracker situation. Help me, Bob.

'Hungry in Plymouth'

Family's important but so is crispy duck. This Friday, take a spoon when you go for the food and help yourself to a couple of generous spoonfuls of duck and a fistful of crackers on the way home. If your mother-in-law complains about the missing food, say it was the 'angel's share'. If she complains again, just tell her to leave.

————————

Dear Bob,

My wife wants me to join her book club. Help.

Joey C, Shoreditch

Sorry, I refuse to discuss book clubs after one was responsible for one of my greatest stitch-ups.[4]

---

4   Quick bit of trivia from long days searching *Dundee Courier* archives for this book: 'Bob Servant' has more mentions in the archives than 'Jesus Christ'.

ANOTHER SAD CHAPTER FOR SERVANT

Fine for Broughty businessman who exposed himself at book club

Broughty Ferry businessman Bob Servant has been in hot water again, after attending a local book club naked following a 'genuine misunderstanding.' At Dundee Sherriff Court yesterday Servant debated at length with Magistrate Narey about what transpired in Broughty Ferry last Wednesday.

"Erotic Code"

The incident began when Servant met a local woman in the plumber merchants on Broughty Ferry's Grey Street while looking for a 'plunger, no pun intended'. Servant explained the woman told him she couldn't go 'for her tea' with him that evening because she was attending a local book club. Servant explained to Magistrate Narey that he felt the woman had been 'giving him the eye' and the 'whole book club thing' was 'an erotic code'.

"Fig Leaf"

That evening, members of Broughty Ferry book club were having a measured discussion on the latest Ken Follett when Servant was described by one witness to have 'steamrolled' into the house in a naked state. On this point, Servant debated at particular length with Magistrate Narey. Servant explained he was in fact wearing a couple of pages of one of his own books over his genitals as 'a sort of fig leaf' and an 'in joke'.

"Wontons"

Magistrate Narey argued that Servant was still exposed. Servant argued that he had a page 'wrapped round my old boy' and two others individually wrapped around his testicles and secured at the 'stem' of the testicle with an elastic band. 'They were essentially like wontons,' explained Servant, 'testicle wontons.' Servant was fined £50. He asked the judge if he could 'pay in book tokens', then dissolved into a hysterical state. He was fined an extra £15 for contempt of court.

Hello Bob,

My husband recently made a joke at a party and got a mediocre laugh and it's all gone to his head. He's not a funny man, Bob, but he's carrying on like he's Billy Connolly. How do I get him to go easy with the 'jokes'?

'We've Created a Monster', Lerwick, Shetland

This happened with Frank in the nineties. He made a joke at Safeways and a passing postman laughed. For a week Frank thought he was Tommy Cooper until I discovered to my relief the postie had been sectioned. You need to find a way to have everyone who laughed at your husband's joke sectioned. It may cause them minor inconvenience but if it makes your husband give up the gags then it's more than worth it.

———————

Dear Bob,

My daughter's announced she wants a horse for Christmas. We live in a top-floor flat. How do we let the wee soul down gently?

Oonagh M, Dublin

The best way to dissuade a child from a pet request is to try and explain how much work is involved. It sounds like your daughter just won't be told so you're going to have to up your game. I suggest you and your husband surprise her on Christmas morning hidden inside a pantomime-horse costume. Stay in character for the next few hours, knocking over furniture and taking it in turns to go to the toilet 'horse style' around the flat. Fairly soon, your daughter will have seen the error of her ways and you and your husband can get Christmas started with a well-earned buck's fizz (pun intended).

Dear Bob,

Our son is falling in with a rough crowd. I'm a bag of nerves and his dad's hopeless, as always. What can we do?

Brenda D, Bolton

Your son is quite rightly seeking the exciting, edgy atmosphere that you and your husband are clearly failing to provide at home. One obvious path would be to give your house a 'jailhouse' atmosphere. Put up posters of near-naked women, and give each other risqué prison nicknames such as 'Skull Crusher' and 'Brenda Boob Muncher'. Your delighted son will soon realise he doesn't have to leave home to find the gritty behaviour he craves.

Good Morning Bob,

Our boy won't let me watch him play football; he says I get 'too angry' after I had a (well-deserved) pop at the referee last week. He'll let his mum go but I've been red carded. How can I talk him round?

'Sinbinned', Norwich

Simply attend the next game as your wife, wearing her clothes, a suitable wig and imitating her voice. Your son will admire your initiative and be pleased as punch to have you back on the touchlines cheering on him and his pals.

Bob,

My husband's started going to karate. He's 52 years old and works on the buses. What's he up to?

'Suspicious Mind', Stirling

Your husband is planning to commit a major crime, probably involving his bus. One for the constabulary, I'm afraid.

Bob,

My son told me the other day that he wants to be Prime Minister. The problem is, Bob, he's a cracking kid and all that but he's really not the sharpest. Do I keep his Downing Street dream alive or try and snuff it out now? Should a parent encourage a kid's dreams when they're totally unrealistic?

'Worried Dad', Arundel

Let me tell you a story about my old schoolmate Sausage McCafferty, a good kid but dare I say not the brightest (sorry, Sausage!). One day his dad, Sausage Senior, asked wee Sausage what he wanted to be when he grew up. Wee Sausage said he didn't know so his dad took him out to the garden and pointed up at the moon. Sausage Senior told his wee boy about the moon landings, the Apollo missions and the footprints the astronauts left in the moon's dust. And he told wee Sausage that some of those astronauts weren't the brightest at school either, but they worked and they worked and one day they flew into space. And do you know what wee Sausage, who everyone had written off, do you know what he ended up doing? He's a plumber. And he's shit at it.[5]

---

5   See *Dundee Yellow* Pages, p.162: McCafferty's Plumbers – 'We'll Certainly Have a Crack at It!'

Health

Bob,

My wife has put me on a health kick. It's all salads and vegetables. What's going on? I'm starving and confused.

'Ravenous', Cambridge

Sorry, pal, there's no sugar coating (pun intended) this one. Your wife's having an affair with a greengrocer. Apply for divorce. Don't bother confronting the greengrocer, I know from bitter experience they are horrifically arrogant with a love of innuendo and, God knows, he'll have the vegetable props close to hand to take full advantage of the situation.

———

Dear Bob,

I am slightly concerned my hairline is starting to slip back. I looked online and there's various potions and whatnot but I thought you might have a better solution.

'Hair Today Gone Tomorrow?', Earlsfield

I do. Reverse any hairline slippage by simply shaving off your eyebrows and then painting them back on a little higher up your forehead. However, be careful not to leave too much of a gap between your eyes and your new eyebrows, or you will look permanently surprised, which could lead to difficulties in social situations and be harmful at work, particularly if you're a doctor and often have to open test results in front of nervous patients.

Hey Bob,

I'm training to do the Great Scottish Run. Any tips to get into peak physical shape?

Lucy B, Aberfeldy

The best way to get good at the running is to be chased. I'd suggest poking a postie until he snaps (make sure he doesn't have a bike) or hurling abuse at a portly pub bouncer (make sure he doesn't have a bike).

Bob,

My wife has an annoying laugh. Is this something an operation could fix? Even if it was an extremely high-risk operation I'd be happy to book her in for it because it's really getting me down. I wouldn't even mind giving her a lift to the hospital, although if I'm busy then it's a pretty straightforward three-bus journey. And I'd give her some money for lunch, if I had the right change.

'No Laughing Matter', Worcester

Firstly, your sense of marital duty is admirable. With sky-high divorce rates it's heart-warming to know that there are still good men like yourself selflessly looking out for your better halves. Unfortunately the NHS do not offer skirt-laugh-fixing operations for reasons (you've guessed it) of political correctness. I'm afraid you'll have to take to wearing a Walkman and, if she's a fan of that all-too-common skirt manoeuvre of throwing her head back like a donkey when she laughs, also a blindfold. Navigating your house in a blindfold and a Walkman may be fairly treacherous, but it's better than the horrific alternative of listening to your wife claw some fleeting enjoyment from her life with you.

Bob,

I have a rash on my leg that makes my skin look like salami, much to the amusement of my flatmates. As a student, I don't particularly like leaving the house, but should I go to the doctor? It's starting to go a bit green.

Tony D, Manchester

No easy way to say it, Tony, it's an amputation job. Get your flatmates to remove it with a bread knife. At worst, you'll feel a slight 'pinch'. And look on the bright side, you've just doubled the size of your shoe collection. Happy hopping.

Bob,

My husband says I'm mad because I like to check all the windows every time I leave the house. It made me think about madness and how one man's madness could be another man's eccentricities. It also, Bob, made me think about you. I hope I don't cause any offence by asking – Bob Servant, are you a madman?

'Insane in the Membrane', Bristol

Firstly, the only way you could cause me genuine offence would be to come to my van and make fun of me in front of my customers, perhaps by saying that my hair looks like lady hair. It doesn't, although on a windy day I accept that the joke would at least make sense. More importantly, you have certainly not caused offence by asking if I'm mad because I know for a fact that I'm not. I was examined by a shrink in the late eighties after a daft misunderstanding in Safeways. Needless to say, I passed with flying colours.

Psychological report

Date 3.3.89

Examiner	Dr R. Milne, MSc MB BCh MRCPsych
Subject Name	Bob Servant (when asked to confirm his name Subject accused me of 'putting words in his mouth').
Date of Birth	Unconfirmed (Subject said I was trying to 'typecast' him).
Reason for Report	Report is court-ordered after the Subject was arrested for suspected exposure in Safeway.

Initial Assessment:

The Subject arrived extremely agitated. He believed that this was a 'travesty' and an unsuitable punishment for what had been 'a joke, and a good one at that'. The Subject explained he had attempted to push a supermarket marrow through the zip of his corduroy trousers 'for a laugh', which had been harder than he realised and led to him accidentally baring his rear end to other shoppers, 'Which was literally the last thing I intended to happen.'

Examination

I asked the Subject the standard questions of the NHS psychiatric assessment.

The Subject gave a stock answer to the first eight questions of 'Wouldn't you like to know?'

When asked if he'd ever had homicidal tendencies the Subject replied he 'once saw a guy at the swimming baths with big muscles and I sort of wanted to prod his muscles to see if they were real but that hardly means I was up for any saucy stuff. I just genuinely wasn't sure if his muscles were real or not. It wasn't like he had his old boy out and I was foaming at the mouth.'

When asked if he'd ever had suicidal tendencies, the Subject replied, 'I met a

Continued over page.

woman on the beach once who said she was a chiropractor. I told a long, yet well-paced anecdote about my feet. She said I was thinking of a chiropodist.

'My walk home felt like I was hiking the Khyber Pass. That night I stared at myself in the mirror for a long, long time. Was I close to taking the easy way out? Hard to say. In the end I cooked myself a bowl of sausages and watched Beverly Hills Cop.'

When asked if he'd ever heard voices, the Subject replied only when he 'listened to my Walkman'.

The Subject then interrupted my next question to make sure I'd appreciated that he had been making a joke in his previous answer.

The Subject interrupted my next question to say, 'I don't know why I bother.' The Subject suggested that rather than examining him, 'Why don't you examine yourself and try to find a sense of fucking humour?' The Subject stood up and said he was terminating the appointment early.

Five minutes later, the Subject returned and asks if he could borrow my stethoscope. He got angry at my refusal and said I was 'a quack'.

Five minutes later, I observed the Subject crawling into my office in an attempt to steal my stethoscope. I greeted the Subject, at which point he adopted a Spanish-style accent and insisted he was a man called 'Julio'. The Subject then crawled backwards from my office explaining he was 'off to see his Spanish wife, Julia'. I observed it must be confusing having such similar names. The Subject muttered something indecipherable and left.

Bob,

Every Thursday evening I play darts at the ex-servicemen's club with my friend Razor (Ray to his mother) so on Friday mornings I often find myself with a crippling hangover. While going to work on a packed Lothian Bus full of squealing school kids this morning, I had a thought, is there any way I could be taken to work in an ambulance? Just on Friday mornings and just when my hangover's particularly bad (i.e. when Razor makes me drink 'doubles for doubles'). I got really into the fantasy of lying on a stretcher while a comely female paramedic lightly dabs my forehead with a wet cloth and tells me that everything's going to be OK. Is this just a fantasy, Bob? I suppose some might argue it's a waste of resources.

'Double Tops', Edinburgh

Firstly, it's certainly not a waste of resources, so get that nonsense out of your head straight away. The NHS is set up with the sole purpose of making the punters feel better and if you're walking about with your head minced with the booze then that is exactly the type of situation the NHS is meant to deal with as a matter of urgency.

Next time you and Razor lose your minds at the oche, simply call 999 and explain your situation. If anything the operator will welcome a break from endless calls about 'So-and-so nicked my umbrella' or 'I think my dad's a gangster.' They'll happily send an ambulance to carry you and your banjoed head to work, and the paramedics will be delighted to have a break from helping grannies find their glasses and rescuing kittens from trees. Your plan is literally flawless. It is, and I think I've got this right, a win-win-win-win-win.

Dear Bob,

My husband's decided to 'get in shape'. He does this every January and it's deeply worrying. He did a sit-up in the kitchen the other

day and nearly dislodged the fish tank. Now he's jogging about in shorts that leave little to the imagination. How do I get him to ease up?

Cathy P, Chichester

I think both you and the fish should take a long hard look at yourselves. Here he is trying to toughen up, and you just throw it back in his face. As for the shorts, think of your husband's bits and pieces as an artwork and the shorts as a picture frame. When he jogs he is exhibiting his masterpiece to the punters, and he, they, and indeed the fish will be all the better for it.

Bob,

It's hard being a woman with all the body shaming and whatnot. As someone who's starting to get bit nervous about the beach, can you tell me what is the perfect diet? Does it even exist?

'Bikini Shy', Liverpool

Find enclosed the Bob Servant diet. Please send £8.99 by return of post.

Stayin' (staying) Alive
with the
Bob Servant Diet!

SUGAR — Sugar is an important part of your diet as it gives you that all important "zip" as you go about your day. The best types of sugar are toffee apples and Terry's Chocolate Oranges, which both count towards your "Five a Day".

POTATOES — Chips are the healthiest way to eat potatoes because you just pop 'em (them) in your mouth without a second thought. Mashed potatoes are a slightly infantile way to eat potatoes. Baked potatoes are fine but suggest you have a lot of time on your hands and you're less likely to be taken seriously by your peers.

FRUIT — Largely a waste of time.

CHINESE FOOD — The

healthiest type of food comes from the exotic "Far East" and the traditional food of the Chinese people. Their "Seaweed" starter is pure, 100% good stuff (ever seen a fat fish?!), while prawn crackers are healthy as hell (ever seen a fat prawn?!).

VARIETY PACKS OF CEREAL —

Just good fun.

CHOCOLATE ECLAIRS —

Delicious and as light as an angel. Scoff them down guilt-free while watching Escape to the Country and feel like the "Lord of the Manor".

BOOZE — You shouldn't really drink

in the mornings unless you genuinely feel that you deserve it. In the evenings NHS guidelines are basically "don't take the piss". A simple rule of thumb is, can you get to your bed without being helped by more than one person? If so, you're "good to go". Cheers!

Bob,

I have a rather pronounced nose. How do I minimise any negative effect with the ladies?

Deek McDonnell, Hackney

Thanks for your letter, Deek, or should I say Beak? Just my little joke, Deek, don't be a fanny about it. With regards to your conk situation, it's all about ownership. By addressing the situation head on (pun intended) you can quickly dilute the impact of your massive sniffer. The next time you go for a date, get a friend to come to the bar wearing a very large false nose and position themselves nearby. To the girl you're with, the looming presence of your friend's 'nose' will reduce your nose down to normal size. That is probably, and I do not say this lightly, one of my best ever ideas. The very best of luck to you, God 'nose' you'll need it.

———

Hey Bob,

Since moving to California, my husband has started listening to self-help tapes and says that he's going to 'let life happen around him' and that he's going to give me 'the gift of patience'. What can I give him in return?

Helen D, Los Angeles

A divorce.

———

Alright Bob,

My friend has taken to wearing fake glasses on a night out because he thinks it makes him look intellectual. A couple of problems – the glasses are from Tesco, and the majority of our nights out are

in Airdrie, where we already look like a pair of intellectuals due to us both managing to wear a pair of matching shoes.

Digger K, Airdrie

This reminds me of my whole briefcase farrago in '87. When my Uncle 'Briefcase' McCloud died, there was only one thing I wanted from his estate, his fun-loving Toyota Celica. When his kids selfishly took that for themselves, I was left with his legendary briefcase. It wouldn't open but it didn't need to. It was the height of the eighties 'Yuppie' movement and by carrying around the briefcase I soon gained a reputation in Broughty Ferry as a man who was 'going places'.

Then, one night in Stewpot's Bar, I was chatting to some skirt who was almost literally eating out of my hand when I dropped the briefcase. It split open and revealed around a hundred photos of my uncle in an excitable state. As you can imagine, Digger, it was very, very hard for me to explain the situation. Under the circumstances, I did relatively well. I told the skirt I was a 'cock doctor' and my uncle was one of my clients who had just sent over these photos for urgent examination. 'In fact,' I said, in a flash of genius, 'I should probably crack on with it now.' Sitting in the corner of a crowded pub carefully inspecting photos of your dead uncle's erect penis might be your idea of fun, Digger, but it certainly isn't mine. I hated every minute of those five hours, and the briefcase was bound for the bin.

Bob,

I'm struggling with the high fives. I tried one at our BBQ yesterday with my son's friend and it was absolutely horrific. The atmosphere in the garden afterwards was strained and I ended up just heading upstairs for an early night. I couldn't get to sleep for hours, just constantly replaying it in my mind. Is it a psychological thing, or medical?

'Low Five', Isle of Wight

It's medical. I'd suggest visiting your local A & E department and talking them through this at length, including a full reconstruction of the whole sorry incident. Hopefully they'll be more understanding than my local hospital, who are a bunch of clowns.

HOSPITAL BANS 'PATIENT FROM HELL'

Broughty Ferry businessman Bob Servant has been permanently banned from Ninewells Hospital's Accident & Emergency department after what hospital management called 'a litany of transgressions'. According to the hospital, Servant has been a regular visitor to the ward ever since he had his foot treated following an incident with a cat.

'Zulu'

'After Mr Servant was successfully treated, he told us he liked the "whole vibe" of the hospital and began returning daily,' hospital management told the *Courier*. They allege various forms of unacceptable behaviour from Servant, including repeatedly accusing other patients of being 'at it' and 'pulling an insurance job', attempting to 'heal' patients with 'motivational speeches that appeared to be monologues from the movie Zulu', and upsetting patients by offering unsolicited diagnoses.

'Adios'

According to the hospital, Mr Servant's diagnoses largely took the form of confident predictions of the need for amputation which often 'involved Mr Servant suggesting that patients "say adios" to one of their limbs'. Last night Mr Servant rejected the hospital's claims as 'ludicrous'.

Good Afternoon Bob,

I give my wife breakfast in bed every morning (that's just the kind of guy I am), but recently I've noticed I've been getting breathless from going up the stairs. Is this is any way a reflection of my fitness? I'm only 18 stone.

'Nice and Wheezy', Nottingham

You're obviously a man who looks after himself, so, if anything, it's a reflection on the stairs. The best plan would be to build a little 'pit stop' halfway up the stairs with delicious snacks and a small bar for you to rest up and enjoy the view before continuing on your journey. For added peace of mind, hire a Sherpa to carry the breakfast.

———————

Bob,

What's the longest you've held your breath?

Kevin T, Dulwich

In 1983 I caught a bus from Dundee to Perth with Frank and Slim Smith. I'm not sure if you know Slim, but he weighs 23 stone naked (something that I tragically know for a fact). We'd just cleared the Invergowrie roundabout on the edge of Dundee when Slim Smith whispered, 'It's happening.' Luckily I recognised this as an 'early warning system' and immediately held my breath as Slim committed a grave offence. I sat with my cheeks puffed out like a squirrel and my dignity fully intact, as I saw Frank's eyes fill with tears and other passengers climb over the seats to escape. Slim just read his paper. I held my breath for 15 miles, all the way to Perth. It was a world record but my infamous humility wouldn't let me send in the form.

Hello Bob,

I'm a farmer and it's very hard not to get a 'farmer's tan' while working in the fields. When I go on holiday I look ridiculous. Any wise words?

'Out Here in the Fields', Shropshire

You need to work on a rotation system. One day wear your normal clothes. Then the next day you simply cover up the areas that were exposed yesterday (face, arms, legs) and expose the areas that were covered the day before (torso, genitals, feet). You will end up with a lovely all-over tan and it will add some welcome variety to your wardrobe.

————————

Bob,

We both put on a fair bit of timber over Christmas and are toying with the idea of joining a gym. Are you a gym man, Bob? Any tips for how to behave while there?

Mike and Louise B, Vancouver

A word of warning on this one, gyms are largely run by frustrated policemen and failed Nazis. I was recently banned from Broughty Ferry's 'Dreamboat Muscles' gym for no reason whatsoever. Avoid.

STAFF INCIDENT REPORT FORM

We have suspended the membership of Bob Servant,
Member 8702345 OFF PEAK.

Reason for suspension: Continual transgression of gym rules

Detail:

3/6/15
Mr Servant was observed loudly shouting out names while lifting a set of children's weights. This was distracting for other gym members. Names included Roger Moore, Adolf Hitler and Adrian Chiles.
Mr Servant explained that while lifting weights he liked to think about people who have 'wronged him', for motivational reasons. Despite being asked to stop, Mr Servant continued to shout out names, including Princess Anne, Shabba Ranks and 'the janitor in Safeways who thinks he's in the CIA'.

5/6/15
Mr Servant challenged another client to an arm wrestle. After swiftly losing the arm wrestle, Mr Servant said he had been 'talking to him' and pointed out an elderly gym member. After swiftly losing that arm wrestle, Mr Servant said he had been 'talking to him' and pointed out a member of the gym's Toddler Turbo Class. After swiftly losing that arm wrestle, Mr Servant said the child was 'probably' possessed by the devil. This upset the other members of the Toddler Turbo Class. Mr Servant then attempted to 'exorcise' the child, which caused widespread panic amongst the rest of the Toddler Turbo Class.

8/6/15
Mr Servant arrived at the gym inebriated. After struggling for half an hour with a single weight, Servant accused other gym members of having 'glued this fucker down'. He then approached other gym members and said they 'thought they were the bee's knees' and that they 'wouldn't last ten minutes in a war zone situation'. Mr Servant was later found sleeping in the disabled toilet.

1

9/6/15

Mr Servant approached a gym member lying on a bench and accused him of having 'plastic' muscles 'Sellotaped' to his arms. He suggested that the member believed this made him look 'like James Bond' but in fact only succeeded in making him look 'like a bell end'. When the gym member stood up to discuss the matter further, Mr Servant ran all the way to the male changing room shouting, 'He's got a blade, he's got a blade.'

11/6/15

Mr Servant was observed popping his head into the female Body Pump Class and shouting, 'I wouldn't mind being an exercise cat.' Mr Servant then grew rapidly flustered and said he had meant to say that he wouldn't mind being 'an exercise mat'. Mr Servant was later found shouting at himself in the showers, berating himself for his mistake. This is not the first issue between Mr Servant and the Body Pump Class, who Mr Servant refers to as 'my girls'. This has caused particular problems between Mr Servant and the male members of the Body Pump Class.

13/6/15

We received a complaint that while in the shower Mr Servant had reached over a dividing wall and attempted to shampoo the hair of another gym user. Mr Servant said he was 'just having a laugh' and that we should 'lighten up'.

15/6/15

We received a complaint that while in the swimming pool, Mr Servant had entered the pool wearing a very large wooden 'shark fin' lashed to his back. Mr Servant then had to be rescued from the pool.

17/6/15

We told Mr Servant his membership was being withdrawn with immediate effect. Mr Servant said he was 'just about to tell us he was leaving anyway'. In the hour after Mr Servant's departure, we received several phone calls from a gentleman with a high-pitched voice saying that Mr Servant had just joined his gym and was 'the best customer he'd ever had' and had 'spent about eight grand on snacks'. The unidentified gentleman explained this new gym was owned by a 'professional catwalk model' who had 'taken quite the fancy' to Mr Servant and had asked him to move into her 'penthouse flat' which was located directly above the gym and connected to the gym by sliding down 'a brass pole like firemen have'. The unidentified voice – which had by now dropped several octaves – then made various double entendres about the brass pole, of rapidly decreasing logic.

2

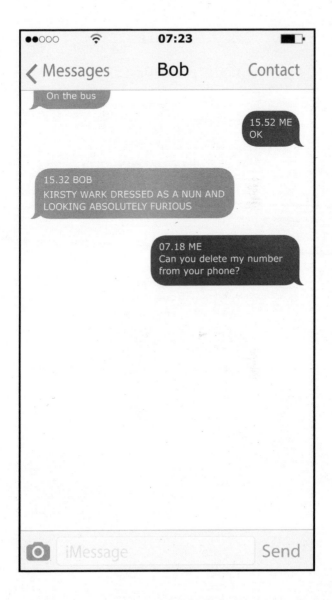

On the bus

15.52 ME
OK

15.32 BOB
KIRSTY WARK DRESSED AS A NUN AND
LOOKING ABSOLUTELY FURIOUS

07.18 ME
Can you delete my number
from your phone?

iMessage   Send

Sex

Dear Bob,

My husband and I work different shifts so our marital relations are limited to the weekends. But he's recently taken to fly fishing on Saturdays and I'm feeling a wee bit neglected. You seem like a man who could help with this delicate matter.

'Frustrated in Berwick'

Marriage is all about compromise and you need to find middle ground between the two pursuits. I suggest surprising your husband on his return from fly fishing by dressing as a sexy Captain Birdseye (lingerie, seafarer's jacket, beard). That will win his attention, then you can hit him with some top-level dirty talk such as 'Here's my catch of the day!' and 'I bet you wouldn't mind getting your hooks into me!' That will lead to a bedroom session that will, possibly literally, take the roof off. Then the two of you can have a nice sit down and watch *Trawlermen* over a bowl of sardines.

Bob,

After logging onto my computer, performing an internet search and then selecting my desired page I was horrified to find that

I'd accidentally stumbled upon a pornographic video. I was even more horrified when I accidentally got an extended look at the anatomies of those involved. On an unrelated note, Bob, what dimensions should a man's 'wand' be? I'm asking, of course, for a friend.

'Concerned (for My Friend)', Hove, Sussex

My rule of thumb (no pun intended) is that a grown-up adult man's old boy should be in the region of a standard-sized Pritt Stick when relaxed, and a jumbo-sized Calypso when in battle mode.

Hi Bob,

At what point during sex should I play the national anthem?

Mike W, Battlefield, Glasgow

At the beginning, then just the chorus at the end.

Bob,

My son's somehow got himself his first girlfriend. As a single mum I'm struggling on the manly advice and I just can't bring myself to have 'the talk'. Can you help?

'Mum's the Word', Oxford

I understand your fears: what if he lets himself down and has a debut to forget? In my day, we picked up snippets about that stuff through old-school pornography kindly left in public parks by well-meaning alcoholics. The best way, and least embarrassing all round, is for you to let your son watch animals copulating. It will feel like an exciting Science project, and you can slip away and let him feast his young eyes on the mind-blowing events in front of him. To ensure it feels 'true to life' I would suggest he watches a muscular horse and a beautifully brushed Shetland pony, or a fun-loving greyhound and a 'dressed up to the nines' French poodle. It all depends on the size of your garden.

Bob,

In your humble though learned opinion, what is the best location for sex?

'Alistair Fresco', Newton Abbot

Performing energetic intercourse amidst the foliage of a heavily wooded roundabout can give the most wonderful thrill. You feel like you're at the centre of the universe, with the whole world spinning round you trying to steal a peak at your genitals. It's like being a major film star living in the Hollywood 'goldfish bowl'. On the downside, it can be quite cold and takes ages to cross the road afterwards.

Bob,

Where do you stand on the whole *Fifty Shades of Grey* phenomenon?

Emily D, Cape Town

I'm absolutely furious about it. In 2005, inspired by real events in my life, I wrote something remarkably similar then left it on a park bench after getting innocently dragged into a situation with a bottle of Tia Maria. It would appear that this *Fifty Shades* woman was walking past, picked it up and nicked the whole shooting match. I suppose in some ways I should be flattered.[6]

---

6   Bob wasn't sure about including the next document, as he feared it would cause an outbreak of 'punters pleasuring themselves in bookshops'.

FIFTY SHADES OF BROUGHTY FERRY

CHAPTER 1 : An Extension Full of Sauce

We shouldn't have been doing this, it was extremely naughty. She was married. And I was supposed to be at the bowling. A play-off with Fintry, for the chance to go up to the Super League.

'Oooh,' she said, 'Nice place you have here.'

'Yes,' I replied, 'It's an extension. Though you wouldn't know it, the way it blends in.'

I'd met the woman earlier that day in Safeways. I made a lengthy but layered joke in the vegetable aisle and she had laughed like a docker. I was delighted, I thought I was alone. She complimented me on the way I was handling a courgette.

'Oooh, ' she said, 'Are you good at handling anything else?'

'Cucumbers,' I replied. 'Or the odd parsnip.'

After a bit more back and forth about bananas, I became aware that the woman was not really talking about bananas but was in fact being highly suggestive. I'm good at picking up signals and I'm all too aware of my effect on women, particularly in Safeways. And particularly in the vegetable section.

So now here we are, back in the extension, saucing things up like we've just got out of prison.

'You're very dirty,' I say to the woman.

'Ooooooh,' she replies, 'Yes I am.'

'You really are' I say, pointing to the mud on her dungarees.

'I've been working on the berries,' she says.

'How much do you get per punnet these days?' I ask.

'15p' she replies. 'Would you like to see my strawberries?'

'Not really,' I say. 'I like blackberries. I'm a blackberry nut.'

'I'd like to see your blackberries,' she says.

'They're not in season,' I reply.

'I'll be the judge of that,' she says, smiling like a murderer.

'I apologise if I've got this wrong,' I say, 'But are you referring to my testicles?'

'Yes I am,' she says, 'I bet they're absolutely mouth-watering.'

'They're just normal testicles,' I tell her, 'Like you see on the TV.'

'Listen,' she says, pointing again to the mud on her dungarees. I'm surprised Safeways let her inside in that state. I once got turned away because my shorts were too snug.

'Maybe you'd like to punish me,' she says, 'For being so dirty?'

'Fair enough,' I reply, 'How about a small fine. Call it a fiver?'

'Is there any other way I could pay,' she asks with a strange smile.

'Well,' I reply, 'I suppose I could take a cheque. Though it seems daft, for such a small amount.'

'Let's get this party started,' she says and right there in the extension, she whips off her jumper.

I look in wonder at what lies beneath. It's another jumper.

'That one will be coming off too,' she says,
'In a bit.'

END OF CHAPTER ONE

Dear Bob,

I read your relationship advice to 'Frustrated in Berwick' with interest. My husband never had much bedroom technique but made up for it with enthusiasm. But now the only thing he seems to have enthusiasm for is you, Bob. He's a huge fan and, to be honest, I think you're affecting our sex life. And not in a good way.

'Agitated of Exeter'

Not surprised to hear this but there's an easy solution. Instead of trying to force me out of your husband's thoughts, simply work me into the equation. Bring back the bedroom magic by wearing a papier-mâché head of myself and, during the action, shout out any of my catchphrases that offer suggestive possibilities, such as 'Grill it on both sides' or 'More sauce, more sauce!' or 'Frank, we're out of change, can you nip over to the newsagent's and split a twenty?'

———————

Hello Bob,

The wife and I were wondering if there are any new positions or techniques we could try when engaging in the sensual arts?

James, Loughborough

In terms of sexual positions then obviously there's the old classics like the Clothes Horse, the Cookie Monster, the Three Point Turn, the Forth Road Bridge, the Enola Gay, the Death Star, the Wheel of Fortune, Blind Man's Delight, the Dual Carriageway and, my personal favourite, the Horse Whisperer. I attach an illustration of the Horse Whisperer and wish you the very best of luck.

Bob,

Thanks so much for the guidance. As you can expect, your illustration got us hot under the collar and we're desperate to give it a go. I'm trying to get hold of a horse that doesn't mind wearing a blindfold and will be willing to sign a confidentiality agreement (not as easy as it sounds) and we did have one other issue. My wife and I were a little confused about the proliferation of legs in the illustration? We're keen to get started before my mother-in-law arrives at the weekend and spoils everything by sitting about doing her Sudoku. Also, I'm afraid I'm not quite as athletic as that–my wife's the gym member.

James

Hello again. Extra legs can be obtained from the mannequins of local department stores, simply explain you require them for erotic purposes, and at worst they'll make you buy a pair of socks. As for your mother-in-law, that should be fine, I've worked her in.

69

Bob,

Many thanks, it was almost exactly as you imagined it. The mother-in-law won't be visiting for a while, but I think the horse had a good time.

James

That's all that matters.

––––––––––––

Hi Bob,

The wife is talking about getting a sex toy. Any thoughts?

Jimbo T, Wolverhampton

Jimbo, you've come to the right place. I invented a sex toy in 1995 and, after a misunderstanding at Safeways with regards to nationwide distribution (never, ever take an order for 1,000 sex toys from a nightshift janitor, he simply doesn't have the authority you'd think he does) they're still in my much-admired 'cantilever' garage. I attach a photo of the 'Orgasmic Infinity'. If it appeals, and I can't see how it wouldn't, then please send a postal order for £8,000.[7]

–––––––––––––––––––––––––––

7   I was once sent by Bob to get a bottle of Tia Maria from his garage. Turning on the light to be met by 1,000 Orgasmic Infinitys was, amidst stiff competition, the most harrowing experience Bob has ever afforded me.

Bob,

This all looks legit and that's obviously a fair price. A couple of quick ones if I may, what is the purpose of the trowel? And is that a photo of Gary Lineker?

Jimbo

Use your imagination and yes.

I'll take two.

Jimbo

Bob,

My boyfriend's started working offshore. We like to think we have a healthy sex life. How do we keep that going with him doing two weeks on, two weeks off?

'Home Alone', Gateshead

You have to employ the magic of phone sex. In 1993 I replied to an advert for a barely used Hoover in the *Dundee Courier* small ads. It belonged to a woman from Forfar who had a voice as smooth as butter. The Hoover had gone but I kept calling her and the next thing you know we had the most torrid session of phone sex. I enjoyed it hugely, though the people waiting to use the phone box were absolutely furious.

Hi Bob,

My neighbours' lovemaking is extremely loud. How do I get them to turn down the dial?

Scott M, Dundee

I had a wee look on the web for you and the loudest lovemaking in the world is performed, presumably with gusto, by the African rhino. Your best course of action would be to pick up a pair of them and keep them in your house. When you get home from work in the evening, work them up into frenzies. The best way to do that is to prance as a 'sexy rhino' with a large horn (no pun intended) and lacy underwear, giving rhino mating calls and asking 'Fancy a bit of this?' in African. After just a few hours of that your rhinos will be primed and ready. As soon as your neighbours get going then simply release the rhinos and give your neighbours a well-earned taste of their own medicine. But make sure you don't get caught in between your new pets in your sexy rhino costume or things could quickly grow nightmarish.

———————

Dear Bob,

I can only get aroused when my girlfriend wears my DJ headphones. She hates dressing up in them though. Help!

DJ Scaramanga Silk, London

I'm surprised and not a little disappointed by your girlfriend's refusal to pop on your workplace outfit in the bedroom. Especially when she's getting off so lightly in only having to wear a set of headphones. Imagine if she was going steady with a deep sea diver, lollipop man or children's clown? She doesn't know how lucky she is, and please make that point to her in terms simple enough for her to understand.

Bob,

I've been asked out by a good-looking lad in the office. When a couple start dating, how long should it take for them to do the act? I'm going to try and play it cool on this one.

'Curious of Leeds'

Try and give it an hour if you can.

Bob,

There are all these pick-up artists about, who strike me as pretty damaged men. But does it work? Is there one sentence you can say to a woman and she's yours?

Ivan F, West Sussex

Yes there is. Simply hold a strand of their hair, enjoy the scent and ask, 'Dare I say, Timotei?' They will, almost literally, melt into your arms.

Hello Bob,

What's the worst thing that's ever happened to you during sex?

Bryn E, London

Actually it happened the day after sex, when a coquettish bus conductress did a classic 'kiss and tell' on me with the snakes at the *Dundee Courier*. Well, she was going to, so I just gave them a ring and got it over with.

WHAM BAM THANK YOU BURGER MAN!

'Servant Made Love All Night' says Bob Servant

Broughty Ferry businessman Bob Servant had a night of torrid passion on Saturday night, according to Broughty Ferry businessman Bob Servant. 'OK, fine,' said Servant this morning, after calling the *Courier* and asking for 'whoever does the filth'. 'Yes, you've got me,' he told us. 'I made love all night long.' Servant explained his partner in the endeavour was a 'bus conductress with a body built for sin, and for working as a bus conductress'.

'God-Given'

'I suppose you perverts won't rest until you get some more details,' continued Servant, unprompted. 'OK, fine. Just write, "Servant was like a wild animal but also surprisingly gentle and with the God-given ability to make just the right joke at just the right time." And call my body a treasure chest,' added Servant, who describes himself as a 'deeply private person'.

'Rock Bottom'

The bus conductress, who asked not to be named, told the *Courier* that she has 'finally hit rock bottom' and that maybe this is 'the wake-up call I need'. Servant described her comments as 'clearly tongue in cheek, pun intended'.

Bob,

What's with the whole dirty-talk stuff? Ever do any of that whilst it's all going off?

'Clean Mouth', Swansea

I never speak to my companion during sex, that just wouldn't feel right, but I speak at length to myself. It's mostly gentle encouragement but I don't 'spare the whip' when I fear I'm letting myself down. There have also been occasions where I've made a particularly good joke and reduced myself to hysterics, which can sometimes cause complications if your partner is suffering from insecurity.

Good Morning Bob,

What is the most attractive you've ever looked?

Steven G, Fife

April 16 1978, or 'Golden Sunday'. I don't know what happened that day but I think about it a lot. I got out of bed and my hair looked 'just right'. I picked up a cardigan and the thing pretty much put itself on. My corduroys seemed to climb my legs like ivy. Then I hit the streets and it was like being at the centre of a skirt hurricane. I got home two days later with frenzied scratches all over my body, but with my dignity fully intact.

Bob,

What kind of background music do you suggest during sex?

'Rump-de-Dump', Cambridge

Marching band music with a firm, unforgiving tempo. Followed by some crooning for when the two of you are relaxing with your sandwiches afterwards.

Hello Bob,

Where do you stand on watching porn as a couple? The wife and I are into it, Bob, there's no point denying it. Some pretty mucky stuff, too, usually over a curry.

Chippy J, Stoke-on-Trent

Chippy, the thought of you and your wife watching hardcore porn while wolfing down a korma in Stoke-on-Trent reminds me of some of the classic scenes of Hollywood's greatest rom-coms. But I'm afraid I'm not a fan of new-age porn. The stories just don't stack up. In contrast, I attach an episode of my creation Bob Sergeant, where you get both the sauce and a gripping story on the side.

THE BOB SERGEANT ADVENTURES
Episode 2 — "Hot, Hot, Hot"

FADE IN:

EXT. STREET. BROUGHTY FERRY.

Bob Sergeant, the Sexy Fireman of Broughty Ferry,
stands looking at a blazing building with some other
FIREMEN (less Sexy).

> FIREMAN
> There's no way Bob. Look at the
> flames. It's Goodnight Vienna for
> any punters in there sadly. God
> bless 'em. Let's just head back to
> the base and play table tennis.

> BOB
> Lads, I didn't sign up to be a
> fireman just so I could drive
> a souped-up bin lorry and wear
> a special helmet.

> ANOTHER FIREMAN
> Come on Bob. Look at the size
> of the blaze. It's massive
> and it's really hot. You'd be
> toasted like bread.

Suddenly a WOMAN'S SCREAM FILLS THE NIGHT AIR.

> BOB
> Did you hear that?

> OTHER FIREMAN (All SHEEPISH)
> I think it was a parrot.

> BOB
> Bollocks it was a parrot. That
> was the unmistakable cry of
> terrified skirt. I'm going in.

All the other FIREMEN try to stop Bob going into the burning building. They say things like "It's not worth it", and
"It's glorified suicide" and "I wouldn't bother myself."
But Bob Sergeant the Sexy Fireman just pops his helmet on
and walks towards the fire and one of the firemen shouts
something again about being toasted like bread and Bob
just laughs and says...

> BOB (CONT'D)
> Well then, someone had better order
> me some strawberry jam.

And he just walks into the burning building like he's popping into Safeways for milk or whatever.

FADE OUT.

END OF PART ONE

ADVERTISEMENT BREAK. - MIGHT BE AN IDEA TO SEE IF ANY FIRE
MANUFACTURERS WOULD LIKE TO TAKE OUT AN ADVERTISEMENT TO
TIE IN. OR THE FIRE BRIGADE MAYBE, BECAUSE IT MIGHT HELP
THEM PRESS-GANG SOME HALFWITS INTO SIGNING UP.

START OF PART TWO

FADE IN:

BOB SERGEANT ENTERS A BURNING ROOM. There's a woman in
there who is top, top, top, top class. Lovely hair, per-
fectly good chin, and a bust that could be heard around the
world. She's also on fire a bit, and I mean that literally.
Bob whips out his hose, no pun intended, and douses her
all over with some cool, refreshing H2O.

> BOB (CONT'D)
> I thought you could do with chilling
> out a bit.

The woman laughs like a drain.

> WOMAN
> Well maybe you could heat me up
> again. If you know what I mean?

>   BOB
>   I know exactly what you mean.
>   The only thing is, the build-
>   ing's on fire. We'd be goners.

>   WOMAN
>   No bother.

Bob Sergeant presses a button and ALL HIS CLOTHES FALL
OFF.

He MAKES LOVE TO THE WOMAN TERRIFICALLY.

NOTE TO DIRECTOR - To show what's going on without
getting too mucky go in and out in soft focus and cut
back to the brass pole at the fire station as a metaphor.
AFTER A RESPECTABLE AMOUNT OF TIME, they wrap things up.
Flames lap at their naked bodies.

>   WOMAN (CONT'D)
>   That was the best thing that's
>   ever happened to me. Which is
>   ironic as dying in a fire is
>   obviously one of the worst.
>   It's bittersweet.

>   BOB
>   Can I ask you a question love?
Bob throws a cigarette up in the air and catches it in
his mouth without even really looking.

>   BOB (CONT'D)
>   I don't suppose you've got a light?

The woman LAUGHS LIKE A MAD WOMAN. Really loud.
CUT TO OUTSIDE THE BUILDING
The woman's laugh drifts out. The OTHER FIREMEN shake
their heads, and smile RUEFULLY.

>   FIREMAN
>   He always leaves 'em laughing.

THE END

Sex

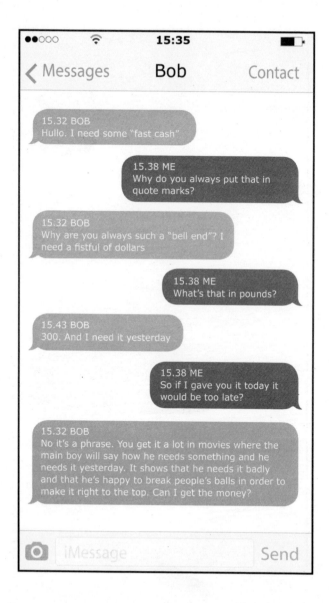

●●○○○ 📶 **15:35** ▬▮

‹ Messages   Bob   Contact

15.32 BOB
Hullo. I need some "fast cash"

15.38 ME
Why do you always put that in
quote marks?

15.32 BOB
Why are you always such a "bell end"? I
need a fistful of dollars

15.38 ME
What's that in pounds?

15.43 BOB
300. And I need it yesterday

15.38 ME
So if I gave you it today it
would be too late?

15.32 BOB
No it's a phrase. You get it a lot in movies where the
main boy will say how he needs something and he
needs it yesterday. It shows that he needs it badly
and that he's happy to break people's balls in order to
make it right to the top. Can I get the money?

📷 iMessage   Send

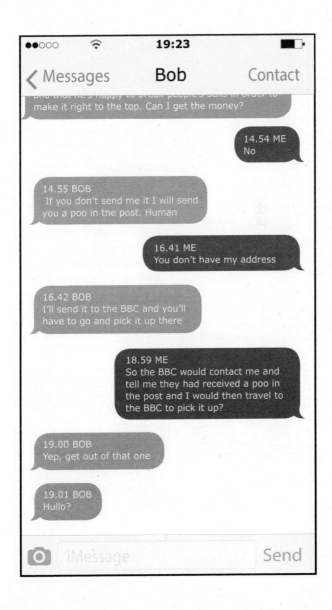

Relationships

Dear Bob,

My wife, by her own admittance, has a helluva temper. How do I calm her when she throws one of her tantrums?

'Ears Aching', Leeds

The easiest way to calm an angry woman is to place your finger on her lips and say, 'You are being utterly ridiculous.' The vast majority of women will instantly fall silent and apologise profusely for their behaviour. If that doesn't work start carrying shiny trinkets in your pockets. When your wife kicks off, take out the trinkets and jiggle them about. She'll be hopelessly entranced and your hell will soon be over.

Bob,

As a recent divorcee my pals are telling me to get back in the saddle, but I've not chatted up a woman for over ten years. Any tips?

'Back in the Game', Glasgow

My main tips would be don't start any sentences with 'as a recent divorcee' or use the phrase 'back in the saddle'. Other than that, just go with the classics. Ask if they've done something extra special with their hair because it looks absolutely fine, or say their make-up doesn't look overly clownish. Either of those openers should see you hovering around a 100 per cent success rate, particularly in Glasgow.

Dear Bob,

I'm getting married in a few months, any pointers for marital life?

Neal D, Sydney, Australia

I've always dodged that particular bullet but my pal Tommy had a wonderful piece of advice, 'Always go to bed on an argument.' No matter what time of day Tommy's wife had a go at him, Tommy would simply pop on his pyjamas and go to bed. It greatly cut down the amount of arguing and worked wonders for Tommy's complexion. Unfortunately, his wife left him for a fun-loving electrician and Tommy now lives in the hostel, where sleeping conditions are a little trickier.

Dear Bob,

I get the bus to work every day and recently there's been the most beautiful woman getting on. I want to go and say hello but I don't know anything about her and fear I'd get tongue-tied and make myself look like a fanny. Any thoughts?

Gaz T, Clapham

Well you know one thing about her, she's a massive bus fan. Simply wheel out some top-level bus-related romance. Something like, 'Excuse me, I'm presuming this bus goes to heaven, because you look like an angel?' or

'May I request a one-way ticket to your heart?' or simply 'I wouldn't mind stamping your ticket.'[8]

Bob,

Manno to manno, is the first date the right time to ask a lass about her deceased husband's power tools? That's not a double entendre, he was a joiner.

Big John, Newcastle

There are fairly strict rules for this and I'm happy to clarify. After a man dies these are the standard lengths of time for asking his wife for his gear. They are: his jokes (a week), his jackets (a month), his dog (three months), power tools (six months) and his ashes (a year, and even then some wives can be a bit 'clingy' on that one).

Hi Bob,

I'm 17 and I think I'm in love for the first time with a girl I met on holiday. But how do I know, Bob? Is love real?

'Young Romantic', Weymouth, Dorset

When you see her do your knees turn to jelly and your eyes go as wide as the Clyde? Does your hair stand on end and your hands crunch into claws? Does your rookie teenage penis start whirling round and round like a tiny wind turbine? Unless all these things happen then it's just a crush that should soon blow over. But, rest assured, love is very real indeed. I've been in love eight times in my life and each occasion has been absolutely wonderful.

---

8   I once witnessed Bob, somewhat manically, deliver these three lines in one bus journey, to three recipients, before he'd taken his seat.

My 'Love Strikes'

1960. Mrs Harrison, Biology. It would never have worked. She was married and I was 14. Yes it was the sixties, but it would have pushed boundaries all over the shop.

1968. A girl on the bus to Fintry.

1978. Safeways, boxed cereal section. A woman with red hair. We spoke for a few minutes until she 'had to go'. Her eyes bore into me like boreholes looking for oil. They found only love. I bought a frozen carbonara and went up the road clutching it to my brow and then pressing it against my troubled crotch.

1989-95. Anneka Rice. When Anneka was up in her chopper on Challenge Anneka, or sexily persuading a local joiner to put up a cupboard for free, I'd be left panting like a hot dog. Once, when she was about to do a swimming challenge in a bikini, I voluntarily knocked myself out to protect my mental health.

1999. Safeways, spring roll section. It was the nineties, 'Britpop' was in its ascendency and I was standing in the spring roll section with my tongue hanging somewhere near my knees. The reason? A heavily made-up woman in a bobble hat. She had just swaggered past me and left in her wake the sweet smell of sweet-smelling perfume. I followed her to the condiments section where she turned to me and said, "Do they have any HP Sauce or is it just this own brand shite?" I swallowed, my voice was as weak as my knees. "Own brand," I whispered. "Fuck that" she said and walked out, kicking over a bin as she went (she was heavily inebriated). It took me four years to get her out of my head. She was my 'own brand'.

2001. Dundee Swimming Baths. Two sisters I met in the queue for the Whip waterslide. Just as I set off on the Whip one of them said "Enjoy the ride". I went down that yellow tube with my mind racing. Was she just a fan of the Whip? Or was she being flirtatious, the way that women always are at council swimming baths? Or had I misheard her? The Whip's acoustics were notoriously bad. Had she said, dare I say it, "I love you"? Did she, did she love me? I was only wearing my second best swimming trunks after the first pair got burnt to cinders in an indoor BBQ fiasco. These ones rode up my thighs and pinched my stomach, giving the false impression that I was seriously overweight. And yet this woman didn't care. She'd taken one look at me, alone at the swimming baths on a Tuesday afternoon and decided, 'I want him and I want him real bad.' When I finally entered the splash pool I was in floods of tears. It was, without doubt, the longest four seconds of my life.

2009. A woman on a late night advert on Channel Four. I think it was for couches or a special type of pyjama. Her arms looked longer than her legs, which flooded my mind with erotic possibilities, though it might have been trick photography or the way she was sitting.

2015. Broughty Ferry Beach. I was lying on my back when an angry woman loomed above me. "Can you keep it down please?" she said. "I think I love you," I replied, quick as a flash. "He's drunk" said the man who loomed beside her. "Why isn't he wearing any trousers?" asked the child who loomed beside him. "Would it be hopelessly inappropriate to say that I have fallen in love with you?" I asked with old-school Hollywood chutzpah. "You're pathetic," said the man. "I wasn't talking to you," I said to the man, "Or you for that matter," I added, to the delinquent child. I closed my eyes and drifted into sleep, my dignity fully intact.

Dear Bob,

Our local postie was an old duffer but he's been replaced with a young Adonis and it's been causing quite the stir. I'm a married woman, Bob, but my pal Jeanie is looking for the best way to approach him. She gets awfully nervous around the menfolk.

'All Aquiver', Dumfries

The best way for your 'friend' to approach the new postie is through the use of double entendre. When faced by a woman skilfully employing a double entendre, every man in the world finds his knees weakening and his business end entering an involuntary spasm. It's one of the main reasons posties do their job. I suggest your friend opens with some 'special delivery' material and slowly steps it up to a level of (almost) unimaginable filth with various plays on her 'letterbox'. That should put her on the right path (pun intended).

Hi Bob,

I have a date tonight. She's coming round for dinner. How about some live Bob Twitter advice during the evening?

@barryspoon, via Twitter

Absolutely.

Barry Spoon @barryspoon
@bobservant Should I wear this shirt?

Bob Servant @bobservant
@barryspoon Only if she lacks the sense of sight.

Barry Spoon @barryspoon
@bobservant She's here.

Bob Servant @bobservant
@barryspoon Good start.

Barry Spoon @barryspoon
@bobservant She's gone to the toilet, running out of small talk, help.

Bob Servant @bobservant
@barryspoon Ask if she had a good time on the toilet and say "It certainly sounded like you did" then send your eyebrows halfway to the moon.

Barry Spoon @barryspoon
@bobservant Didn't go well.

Bob Servant @bobservant
@barryspoon That's unusual.

Barry Spoon @barryspoon
@bobservant She's just said that I've got 'a really nice aura'.

Bob Servant @bobservant
@barryspoon Ask her to leave with immediate effect.

Barry Spoon @barryspoon
@bobservant She's gone.

Bob Servant @bobservant
@barryspoon Thank Christ.

Dear Bob,

I picked up a parking ticket because my new girlfriend spent twice as long as she said she would at the shops. Can I ask her to pay it and how do I go about doing so? I like her but I'm skint.

'Double Yellow', Edinburgh

Suggest some erotic role play where you play the part of a hunky traffic warden giving her a ticket and getting her to write a cheque, then simply pocket the cheque. If she finds out you cashed it just say you did so for an 'added thrill'.

———————

Hello Bob,

My husband's the most unromantic man in Ireland. Can you give him some advice ahead of Valentine's?

Caitlin P, Dublin

My friend Tommy used to have a wonderful Valentine's Day joke with his wife where he'd just give her a fish supper with a bow around it, the joke being she was allergic to fish. It was just a bit of fun that meant they at least got a joke out of an otherwise disappointing evening. And now Tommy lives in the hostel where Valentine's Day isn't even celebrated, so he had the last laugh there.

———————

Alright Bob?

Problems with the wife. She keeps trying to take me up town on a Saturday for some new gear. It's a nightmare. I'm a taxi driver with a generous build so shopping for clothes is a distressing experience.

Big Frankie, The Gorbals

Frankie, a man's wardrobe is his castle. You need to tell your brandy-soaked (a hunch) wife to leave you to it. I wear leather jackets, the international uniform of the maverick, and set them off with a bunnet to show I'm a man of the people. With your build and line of work, Frankie, I'd suggest a terry towelling tracksuit. It's comfortable, it's warm, and more than anything it's a bit of fun.

Bob!

I've just started seeing a guy and it turns out he's a rabid right-winger. But he's very attractive. Oh dear, Bob, what to do?

'Morning Star', London

Get out now before you become his Eva Braun. It didn't exactly work out too well for her. Yes, she got to live in a fun underground den for a bit, but it was a helluva pay off at the end.

Hi Bob,

My wife put my favourite jumper in the wash, now it looks like it belongs to a mouse. Grounds for divorce?

'This is Woolshit!', Burton-on-Trent

Why stop at divorce? This is one for the constabulary. A hard phone call to make, but worth it to take this vindictive, heavy-drinking (an educated guess) maniac off the streets.

Bob,

My boyfriend hasn't proposed. It's been three years. I keep dropping little hints but he doesn't seem to spot them. What do you think?

'Always the Bridesmaid', Toronto

The best way to force his hand is to show him what a wonderful day your wedding would be. When he's at work, create a vision of the wedding. When your ring-shy boyfriend comes back in the door and is met by the sight of you in a wedding dress and your extended families gathered around, his worries about your pushy nature will vanish into thin air and he will almost definitely propose on the spot. It's a fun way of making him think about the situation, but without putting him under any pressure whatsoever.

Dear Bob,

Where do you stand on public displays of affection? My husband is a typical Scot and is not a fan.

'Wandering Hands', London

Get your filthy mitts off him. Sadly, the downside of having a pair of eyes that can twinkle on command is that women have always been keen to fondle me. I've had to lay down fairly strict ground rules. They can fondle me on the Claypotts roundabout in Broughty Ferry during the morning rush hour (to show the rat-race commuter mob how the other half live), in the bedroom (obviously) and in the condiments section at Safeways (so I can make a 'looks like things are getting saucy' joke to other shoppers). Other than that, I have a strict 'paws off' policy and I support your husband in his brave stance. For the removal of doubt, I attach a diagram of where men can be touched by their wives and others.

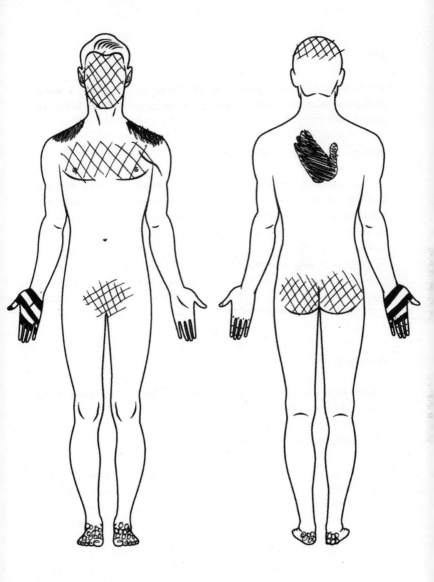

Wife

Male friend

Stranger

shoe salesman

Ask Bob

Bob,

Thirty-year anniversary coming up. My son's arranging a party and my wife wants us to renew our vows. The thing is, Bob, the whole 'Till death do us part' bit got me a little concerned. We're not getting any younger and if my wife shuffles off first then surely, after an appropriate amount of grieving, I'd need someone else to look after me. Maybe a neighbour or something—I can't see me fancying walking too far. How do I show my wife gratitude for the last 30 years, while getting out of the whole 'till death' business without winding her up? You know how sensitive women can be.

'Heaven Can Wait', Cornwall

You've clearly got the whole romance business down pat, but if you'd allow me one suggestion, perhaps give her a sketchbook of your life together. It's a romantic gesture that will soften her up before, through sketches, you skilfully buy yourself a pass for the future. I'd suggest starting the sketches with one of you two meeting, one of your wedding, one of the two of you in the bedroom department, one of her in the act of childbirth, then one of her funeral (make sure you look properly sad in that one), then several sketches of you and your neighbour, both well into your eighties, tentatively exploring each other's aging bodies in the bedroom department. That should give your wife a lovely, and relatively romantic, overview of your feelings. I have a spare childbirth sketch I did for Frank's nephew Tyson's school project so feel free to use that. He doesn't need it anymore, what with the expulsion.

Dear Bob,

Which aisle of the supermarket is the best place to meet new friends?

Bridget K, Scottish Borders

Depends what you're looking for. Traditionally it's the vegetable aisle for romance (high availability of props for saucy suggestions) and anywhere near the fajita packs for that 'Anything can happen' party vibe. What I cannot emphasise enough is do not look to make friends in the car park. I have formed various relationships of various natures in supermarket car parks over the years and it's always the same – they start absolutely superbly and quickly descend into the most horrible levels of bitterness and regret.

———————

Hi Bob,

My wife went to the hairdresser's the other day and came home with an absolute catastrophe. It's all over the shop like she's been attacked by Edward Scissorhands. She looks ridiculous. Should I tell her and what's the best way to do so?

Tinker G, Stockport

Yes, you need to tell her, it's simply the right thing to do. The key is choosing when to do so. By far the best time to tell your wife that you think she looks ridiculous is in the immediate aftermath of a car accident. If that option isn't available then take the sting out of the situation by phoning her work and asking a colleague to pass on the message, or simply whisper it just before she falls asleep.

Bob,

What's the best way to tell a fellow train passenger you're attracted to them?

'Citylinker', Leeds

Morse code blinking.

Hi Bob,

I've texted a girl twice suggesting a date and left her a voicemail. Nothing back. What are the rules on this sort of thing? I imagine you're the man to ask. Is it three and out?

Ali M, Brooklyn, New York

The good news is that you can keep going as long you want. The bad news is that of all the things that can happen as you continue, none of them are very good for you. The worst thing about an extended skirt campaign is the absolute havoc it wreaks on your mind and your ticker. In the late nineties I met the most wonderful piece of skirt at the butcher's in Brook Street and made a joke about seagulls that had her literally vibrating with pleasure. I found out where she lived and sent her a top-drawer bunch of flowers. Nothing. I sent another. Nothing. And so on. To cut a long story short, over the next week she let herself down very badly indeed. I, on the other hand, came out of the process with my dignity intact and very possibly enhanced.

Hullo!
We met at the butchers.
You were wearing a beautiful,
pea-green cagoule and I made a joke about what type
of perfume seagulls wear that had you howling. Would
you like to go out for tea?
You can have anything you want,
within reason.

16.04.98

17.04.98

Hullo again!

Has a cat stolen your tongue?!!!!!!!
In case you were told a few
seagull jokes, mine was
the one that finished with
"Caw Caw Chanel."

As in Coco Chanel
the perfume, so it's
based on the noise
seagulls make.

18.04.78

Who do you think you are?

19.04.78

YOU'D THINK YOU WERE BLOODY ANNIE LENNOX THE WAY YOU'RE CARRYING ON. TOO BUSY ARE YOU PRANCING ABOUT IN YOUR SHITTY ANORAK?

20.04.78

PS Offer still stands for your tea

21.04.78

●●○○○ 📶 **15.52** ▮▮▯

‹ Messages **Bob** Contact

15.12 ME
You seem to have accidentally sent
me a photo of a Flymo lawnmower

Read 15.12

15.20 ME
Hello? Can you send me a photo of
the handheld hovercraft?

Read 15.20

15.32 ME
Can't wait to see it

Read 15.33

15.39 ME
Not sure you're getting these
messages? You're probably
out on your hovercraft

Read 15.39

📷 iMessage Send

Fame

Bob,

What's it like being famous?

Steve R, Wimbledon

To be honest, it's just been more of the same. I've been turning the punters' heads in Broughty Ferry my whole life. During Dundee's Cheeseburger Wars in the eighties, people saw me as a sort of benevolent warlord and flocked to me for protection. When the books and the telly came round it was like some boffins carefully fitted a rocket to my buttocks and sent me to the moon of fame.

There are two downsides to being a household name. Firstly, the whispers. I don't have time to respond to all the rumours about me so let me just say: no, I don't sleep in a bath full of Fanta (why on Earth would I do that?), no, I don't have an artificial neck (how would that even work?), and no, I am not 'romantically involved' with Ewan McGregor (I respect Ewan as an actor but there are no feelings beyond that, at my end anyway).

The second downside to fame is the way that other famous folk hang about with me to try and give a boost to their own careers.

It ain't (isn't) easy being Bob Servant (i.e. me).

Dear Bob,

I was wondering if you could pass on any pearls of wisdom that you may have picked up following your retirement as a cheeseburger magnate. I have recently retired from my profession and so would appreciate any help you can offer.

Cheers,

Chris Hoy[9]

It's a difficult time for us both, Chris. I'm going to miss the roar of the crowd, the adrenalin rush and wearing Lycra. And you'll probably miss getting free puncture repairs for your bicycle. I do, however, have a possible solution. There is a gentlemen's toilet on Broughty Ferry's troubled Brook Street that is lightly used. I propose we buy it from the council and open up Britain's first (and, therefore, best) cycled-powered disco. 'Saddle Up!' will send shockwaves through Broughty Ferry, offering the punters some old-school Hollywood glamour. A jazz band, a rotating dance-floor, barmen covered in feathers and you in the corner going hell for leather on a BMX connected to the mains box. You will, of course, also be covered in feathers. Are you in?

Bob,

Absolutely. It sounds like I'll have my work cut out keeping 'Saddle Up!' in electricity (particularly the rotating dance floor, which will presumably have considerable energy demands). May I ask what your role would be?

Chris

I will be Director of Vibe, working the room and making just the right joke at just the right moment with the punters, seeing VIPs to their tables and occasionally coming over to towel you down (not in a saucy way).

---

9   I should clarify that all notes in this chapter are genuine missives to Bob from those named. Bob has recently taken to referring to his phone as 'Access Hollywood'.

Thanks, Bob. Will I have any sort of break? And what would the profit split be? With all respect, it sounds like I'll be doing the majority of the work.

Chris

Sorry, Chris, no breaks, got to keep the lights on! Every couple of hours, I will oversee one of the barmen carefully feeding a string of sausages into your mouth. I'm afraid that this counts as a 'staff meal' so the meat will be right out of my bottom drawer. Don't worry about toilet breaks either. I have a pair of adapted underpants that will keep you relatively safe. And while the position is unpaid in a financial sense, it will do a huge amount for your profile.

Dear Bob,

I can't thank you enough. Since my retirement, I have had a huge number of employment offers and have waited patiently for the right one. Your suggestion – that I spend my nights working for free, performing a highly strenuous job in a converted public toilet, wearing a homemade nappy, and being fed poor-quality sausages by a man covered in feathers – is undoubtedly the offer that my advisers and I have been waiting for. I'm in.

Chris

Thank you, Chris, I can't see any way that you could ever regret this.

Bob,

As an ex-burger-van operative myself, and one who knows about oppression by the authorities, how did you go about dealing with the local bureaucrats on the council, and specifically the environmental health department? Do you keep it strictly legit in your dealings with them?

Irvine Welsh, Miami

It all comes down to the question, what is a bung? Is it a bung for an Environmental Health Officer to visit the van every lunchtime, only pay for a Kia-Ora, and get a triple-decker meal deal with a fiver hidden in the chips? Is it a bung for me to take him on an all-expenses paid VIP trip to Zapzone and 'play dead' even when he misses me? Is it a bung for me to satisfy his sexual fantasy (being prodded by Frank with a big stick while messing about with himself in a skip behind Safeways) and then to pay for Frank's therapy sessions? The answer to all of the above, Irvine, is a resounding no. I keep it legit.

Thanks, Bob, glad to hear you keep it clean. One question, would the skip experience be available to members of the public? I have a flight to Broughty Ferry on hold.

Irvine

Irvine, board the plane. Frank, sharpen the stick.

Hello Bob,

As a Scottish icon, which other great Scots do you feel the closest affinity to?

Jack Whitehall, London

I'm close to most of the big names. Sean Connery and I have been pals ever since I met him at a jumble sale in St Andrews in 1983. I made a joke about a pair of china dogs (whether or not they produced china excrement) that had Sean weeping with laughter. I've not heard from him since, but we've both been busy.

The Krankies and I had a weekend in Inverness in the early nineties that was, to cut a long story short, like the Last Days of Rome. And Andy Murray and I go way back. I'll never forget watching him hit a few shots when he was just a wee boy. 'That kid's going to be a star,' I said, at which point his mother Judy told me in no uncertain terms to get out of their garden.

I met Sir Alex Ferguson at a motorway service station just outside Carlisle in 2001. I had been in England on a wild goose chase involving an industrial onion slicer and Sir Alex had been 'going somewhere'. We had a good laugh about the fact he 'really had to go' and I did some good physical comedy (standing in front of his car), which brought out some of that trademark, 'angry man' comedy character he does so well. In a flourish that cemented our friendship forever, he treated me to an ironic 'flick of the Vs'.

But, out of all the Scottish big guns, I'm probably closest to Lulu. I really should get in touch.

From: Bob Servant

To: [REDACTED]Management@[REDACTED].com

Subject: For the Attention of the One and Only Lulu!

Lulu,

How are you pal? I'm sure just seeing my name has left your heart fluttering like a butterfly and your eyes spasming with desire! 😍

We met in 1987 (was it really so long ago?) in the car park of the much-admired Little Chef restaurant on the outskirts of Dundee. You were on your way to a (no doubt show-stopping) performance in Glasgow, and I had just been to see a second-hand wardrobe in Invergowrie (waste of time, was missing a drawer, to not mention in a small ad that a wardrobe is missing a drawer should be a criminal offence). 😡

We chatted for a while about your career and I gave you some advice (lift your chin a little more, and open your mouth wider during the chorus, you've got a top level set of gnashers, so let the punters see them!) Then we talked about the wardrobe and the conversation became somewhat overladen with double entendres. 💜

You said you were 'running late' and looked (almost) tearful at leaving me. As you were driven away I lifted one hand in a clenched fist gesture, the classic greeting of Broughty Ferry burger van workers and our brethren in the American Black Panthers. You looked sad. ☹️

It was a meeting that, in many ways, changed my life and I hope I'm not being presumptive to suggest it probably did the same for you. I think of it and you on an (almost) daily level, do you ever think of me? 👀

Your 'Pal in the Car Park' 👄

Bob Servant 👿

From: [REDACTED]Management@[REDACTED].com

To: Bob Servant

Subject: re: For the Attention of the One and Only Lulu

Thanks for your email. Lulu loves hearing from her fans. She is currently recording her new album. Please follow her website for updates.

From: Bob Servant

To: Jack Whitehall

Subject: FW: For the Attention of the One and Only Lulu

Jack,

See the attached. Interesting stuff. Lulu 'loves' me (L bomb alert!)
She wants me to 'follow' her. And if I know a little about entendres
(and I know a lot about entendres) then the whole 'recording her new
album' stuff is absolutely dripping in it. Thoughts?

From: Jack Whitehall

To: Bob Servant

Maybe go to the recording studio and pop out of a cake naked? Knowing
Lulu as I do, she'll love it.

From: Bob Servant

To: Jack Whitehall

BEEN ARRESTED AT THE RECORDING STUDIO COULDN'T GET A CAKE BIG ENOUGH
SO JUST SORT OF HELD SOME DOUGHNUTS IN FRONT OF MY OLD BOY AND
SHOUTED SURPRISE NEED HELP URGENTLY NICE IDEA YOU FUCKING IDIOT

From: Jack Whitehall

To: Bob Servant

This email address is no longer in use.

Bob,

Would you like to buy *Jurassic Park* **on LaserDisc?**

Sanjeev Kohli

No.

Dear Bob,

I'm a member of a popular beat combo and spend a lot of time on the road. I often think fondly about my childhood home of Fife. As someone who lives just over the river and probably spends a lot of time admiring Fife, what's been your favourite trip over the river?

Guy Berryman, Coldplay

Nice try. As I suspect you well know, I am not a Fife fan. I find the natives unbearably arrogant, and entirely unresponsive to well-worked jokes. But I'll play your game. On a rainy day in 1993 I was tempted to drive to Fife to purchase a competitively priced, fire-damaged clock radio. My van broke down on the Tay Bridge. I was inspecting it when a passing lorry driver threw a half-eaten sausage supper that hit me in the face. I then realised I was locked out the van. I stood waiting in the rain for the AA, during which time another passing lorry driver threw a half-eaten mince roll that also hit me in the face. The van needed to be towed and I walked home to Broughty Ferry. While walking along the Dundee Road, a passing lorry driver threw a half-eaten lamb vindaloo that hit me in the face and caused temporary blindness to go with the pneumonia. I was in bed for a week. That was, without doubt, my favourite trip to Fife.

Bob,

Please settle an argument between my postie and me. How long should sex last?

Yours respectfully,

John Niven, Bucks

An easy way to gauge it is to pop on an egg just before you start. Ideally you want to be looking at a hard-boiled situation but, as long as it's edible, you've done fine.

Greetings Bob,

You obviously have extensive experience in the burger industry, and it seems now with the introduction of the 'gourmet' burger, that market seems to be ever expanding. Are you tempted to enter the gourmet-burger world?

Greg McHugh

My friend, I invented the gourmet-burger world. I launched my first during the Falklands (the 'Belgrano') and ever since then have thrilled the punters with a conveyor belt of exotic concoctions and 'lifestyle packages' such as our popular 'Divorcee Special' (burger, chips, mug of gin and small bottle of mascara).

Our bestselling burgers are the classic 'Widow Maker' and our newly launched 'Computer Burger', which, as part of our modernising drive, can be ordered on the World Wide Web. You just 'email' Frank's nephew Tyson saying when you'll be down, and he simply catches two buses to the harbour, jogs over to the van and lets us know. I attach my much-admired posters. Frank sometimes moans I put too much into the poster budget but it's worth every penny to keep us looking cutting-edge.

Dear Bob,

As a proud Dundonian who sadly got dragged away from the city with work, I often think back fondly to my younger years. And, in doing so, I remembered with some horror that we have met. 1959, the Forte's ice-cream parlour in Dura Street. You had a double cone (both sides vanilla, showing a lack of imagination) that had dripped down your cardigan. I remember you were a curious-looking wee boy, with a runny nose, and seemed to find it hard to communicate with women. Have things improved at all for you or, God forbid, got worse?

Brian Cox, Brooklyn, New York

You've got a bloody nerve, Coxy. I remember that day well. You were clumsily chatting to some girls when I strolled over and made one of my first and (arguably) best pieces of double entendre in a well-worked joke about flakes. The girls laughed so hard their eyes bulged up like marbles and a passer-by introduced himself as a top Hollywood Showbiz Manager and asked if I wanted to go to Hollywood with him 'right here, right now'. I said, 'No, my work in Dundee is a long way from being done.' He then turned to you and said, 'I suppose you'll do.' I walked away with my head held high, leaving the girls panting like dogs in my wake and your eyes brimming with jealous tears.

Bob,

We're both of a healthy age yet it would appear that your memory is starting to fail first. I was doing absolutely fine with the girls (in fact we were lining up a game of kiss chasie round the Stobie Ponds for later that afternoon, and you know as well as I do that a game of kiss chasie round the Stobie Ponds can be a far from innocent experience). You then interrupted and told your so-called 'joke' that failed on several fronts (logic, delivery, humour), leaving me to cause a diversion by bursting into song, which attracted the appreciative attention of the aforementioned Hollywood bigwig. You went up the road with your tail between your legs and I remember thinking that I would read about you

one day in the *Dundee Courier*. **I presumed you'd be arrested for an amateur-ish confidence trick or suchlike, so well done on surpassing my meagre expectations.**

Brian

I think we're going to have to agree to disagree on this one, Coxy. The important thing, of course, is that we remain pals.

I think let's go for 'associates'.

Can I come and visit you in America?

No.

Dear Bob,

I'm looking for some advice on my upcoming wedding. As an actor people are expecting a first-class groom's speech but, as I usually have my lines written for me, I'm a tad nervous. I was hoping a well-renowned public speaker such as yourself could give me some tips on winning over a crowd?

Much appreciated,

Martin Compston, Greenock

A lot of people get the groom speech all wrong. They think they have to bang on about the bride, how she's one of the good guys and a safe pair of hands and so on, but that only serves to make the groom look desperately weak. The groom's speech is a chance to show the bride's family that you are a strong man, willing to make brave choices and stand up for yourself. It's absolutely vital you hit the ground running, and the best way to do that is to open your speech with a sustained attack of bawdy jokes on an elderly relative on your wife's side. A 'shock and awe' onslaught against this kindly and entirely innocent individual will show the guests that you are your own man. They'll hand you an ovation that you will never forget while your wife simpers with delight at your daring.

Bob,

What would be your dream cheeseburger dinner-party line-up, living or dead?

Much love,

Rufus Jones, London

The classic cheeseburger-van conundrum, I've been debating this one for years. Right now, I think I'd plump for famous petrol-head Nigel Mansell, wrestling great Big Daddy, actress Whoopi Goldberg and former Iraqi head-honcho Saddam Hussein. I'd like to pick Nigel's brain about burger-van turning circles and compare notes with Big Daddy on his 'oh so familiar' showman abilities. I would greatly enjoy chatting to Whoopi about her varied career, while Saddam would provide security as well as (hopefully!) treating us to his trademark dry wit.

Dear Bob,

I see Dundee are embarking on a multi-million pound redevelopment of the Waterfront. I presume this will feature a statue of your good self?

Your servant,

Jonathan Watson

What a wonderful idea.

From: Bob Servant

To: Dundee City Council

Subject: Let's Shake Things Up A Wee Bit Here

To whom it may concern,

I have a suggestion for the Waterfront development. It is, you might
have guessed, a statue of myself. The design is simple and, most
importantly, has a twist. The statue will be of me right on the
riverfront, bending over towards Dundee and accepting a bunch of
flowers from a child. This shows me as a kindly uncle (the good type),
a man of the people, being recognised by grateful Dundonians for my
service to the city.

Behind, over my much-admired rear end, my corduroys should be
loosened to my knees, as I send a message to Fife on behalf of Dundee
that will be frozen in bronze for eternity. I enclose a sketch, and
look forward to your acceptance of my proposal,

Your Servant,

Bob Servant

PS This idea was entirely that of the Glaswegian actor Jonathan
Watson.

From: Dundee City Council

To: Bob Servant

Subject: re: Let's Shake Things Up A Wee Bit Here

Many thanks for your interesting suggestion. I'm afraid the
Waterfront has now been fully designed and we hope you enjoy seeing
the project come together.

Jonathan,

See the attached. I'm afraid they didn't go for your idea.

Bob

Thanks Bob,

A lot of actors manage their public personae quite carefully, being tight-lipped in interviews and spending their careers carefully avoiding controversy. I, on the other hand, have always felt a better course of action would be agreeing to be the public face of an exchange with a local authority where I suggest the building of a pornographic statue. Thanks for giving me the opportunity.

Yours respectfully,

Jonathan

Dear Bob,

I am in a six-piece combo band in the Glasgow area and we're looking to take the next step up. We've just finished a two-week residency that saw us sell out both the lounge and bar area of Cathcart Bowling Club. Willie McKerlin (promoter for said venue) says he's never seen anything like it since Peter Smith and the Jackets in '83.

Clearly we've gone as far as we can go in Glasgow, and we now want to crack the lucrative East Coast market. We're talking, of course, about Broughty Ferry. We're also looking to leave our current management, Shug McPherson Entertainment, for a more experienced manager. Would you be interested in managing us, Bob? I've heard you're the Colonel Tom of the East Coast, the Brian Epstein of the Ferry. Please help.

Richard (drummer), Belle and Sebastian

Richard,

Yes, I am available to be your Svengali, but with some fairly straightforward conditions:-

1. Most of the time, I will reward you with individual arms round the shoulders and gentle encouragement. However, when I think it is necessary, I will also give each of you an absolute rocket. For maximum effect, these rockets will come with the element of surprise, for example when you are sleeping, or using the lavatory. They will be deeply uncomfortable situations for us both but will be to the long-term benefit of the band, and that's my only concern.

2. Quite rightly, you lot will get all the plaudits, the glory and an industrial quantity of skirt. In return, all I ask is that I, quite rightly, get all the money.

3. Congratulations, you've got a new opening act – Bob and Sebastian. Sebastian is my friend Slim Smith's cocker spaniel. We'll take to the stage as a fun icebreaker before you go on. I'll talk about funny things that have happened while I have been in Sebastian's company, and Sebastian will roll his eyes during the punchlines.

4. Album covers will be me doing the splits in leather trousers and my hair worn in a rock 'n' (and) roll 'quiff' style.

5. The tour bus. Downstairs will be kitchen, bathroom and some 'bucket seats' for the band. Upstairs will be Bob's No-Rules Party Zone (NRPZ). After a gig, I will invite you and any VIPs up to the NRPZ for some unrestrained rock 'n' (and) roll madness – telling rude limericks, giving each other love bites, eating jelly with our hands, etc.

6. Every song on the albums will end with me saying, 'And that's that!'

Bob

Bob,

I'm delighted to say that it's a deal. We got instant approval for your demands from our music lawyer, Dykes McPherson. Dykes is actually a boiler engineer but was once in a band called Scenario Terra Firma (STF) and negotiated a record contract for the band with Pye Roll records. Unfortunately, the label was sued for using a similar name to another record company and the band broke up after one cassette single with the chart-friendly title 'I'd Rather Keep You for a Week than a Fortnight'. Dykes has never really got over it, as you can imagine. Would there be a role for him in your organisation?

Richard

Would he consider spending his days grooming Sebastian and his evenings picking up any 'deposits' that Sebastian or (God forbid) the band make on stage?

Bob,

I know for a fact that he would.

Richard

He's in. See you Monday. Bring your instruments and an open mind.

Bob

Dear Bob,

It's not easy being a Brit marooned in France. For example, why is it the French make top-of-the-range bread, but when it comes to marmalade they are total rubbish? All my French pals ask me to get jars of Dundee marmalade when I pop back to the UK. Do you travel yourself, Bob? I expect the marmalade fiasco is the type of thing that persuades you to stay in Blighty.

Barry Fantoni, Calais

You're spot on, Baz, I've got no time for the foreign-holiday mob. They come back to Scotland drinking Lilt and making out they're Christopher Columbus because they went to Magaluf for ten days. Frank and I are eyeing up a long weekend at the static caravan in Pitlochry but I'm in two minds. Last time we went Frank was a nightmare, moaning about how the milk tastes different and the locals look like they'd 'perv' on his wife if he were married and she was there with him. We'll probably just go for the day.

Bob,

You're obviously an inspiration to many, but who is your inspiration?

Yours with deepest respect,

Gordon Smart, Kinross

Churchill, Mandela, Humperdinck.

Dear Bob,

Perhaps you might offer advice on a delicate matter. Having been married for 40-odd years, I'm beginning to find my wife's lack of enthusiasm in the boudoir department something of a problem. My recent attempts to spice things up have met with little enthusiasm, particularly after I coaxed her into attempting the 'wheelbarrow' position (she still can't wear a low-cut dress due to the carpet burns). The final nail in the coffin was a recent conjugal session when I asked her to rustle up some enthusiasm and suggested she could try a wee bit of moaning.

'Well, alright,' she replied, 'if that's what you'd like.' As the point of no return approached, she asked if I wanted her to start. I agreed and she said, 'So when are you gonnae put up them bloody shelves in the kitchen?'

Any advice in rekindling a flame from the dying embers of our once-passionate love life would be appreciated. It goes without saying that since I don't want my small-but-loyal army of elderly fans tittering amongst themselves at *Taggart* conventions, perhaps in the book you can refer to me using a nickname.

Sincerely,

Alex 'A Nickname' Norton, Languedoc, France

Firstly, happy to help on the nickname front, though I'm not entirely clear how that will help on the tittering front. Secondly, to help bring the fireworks back, I would suggest you and your wife consider the perusal of erotic material with a strong central character and a believable story. In fact, I've got just the thing.

THE BOB SERGEANT ADVENTURES
Episode 3 — "FACE OFF"

FADE IN:

INT. HOSPITAL CORRIDOR. NEW YORK CITY.

                    ORDERLY
          Get outta the way! Get outta the
          Goddamn way!

The 'ER' orderlies run through the hospital pushing a
trolley with a beautiful woman on it. She's covered in
blood. She's had a bad time.

                    ORDERLY (CONT'D)
          Get outta the Goddamn way!

INT. SURGERY THEATRE. SAME TIME

In the Hospital's Surgery Theatre, BOB SERGEANT, the
Sexy Plastic surgeon of Broughty Ferry sits patting his
German Shepherd BARTHOLOMEW on the head.

                    BOB SERGEANT
          You're a helluva dog Bartholomew,
          a helluva dog.

Bob Sergeant's eating a cucumber sandwich. No crust.
Bartholomew ate earlier.

SUDDENLY the orderlies use the trolley to BURST OPEN
the doors to the Surgery Theatre.

                    BOB SERGEANT (CONT'D)
          What'cha got boys?

Bob Sergeant is 'Trans-Atlantic'. Most of the time he
works in Broughty Ferry but today he's working in the
one and only NEW YORK CITY.

                         ORDERLY
              She's bashed up real good Surgeon
              Sergeant. Gawd bless 'er.

Bob Sergeant takes off his fedora and throws it across
the room. It lands on the hook. Bullseye.

                       BOB SERGEANT
              What the hell happened to her?

                         ORDERLY
              She fell down some stairs.

                       BOB SERGEANT
              Oh yeah? Where? The Empire State
              Building?

The ORDERLIES LAUGH like madmen. One of them urinates
all over the floor.

                   BOB SERGEANT (CONT'D)
              OK, OK, OK, OK, OK, let's get to
              work. Clean up that urine and mop
              up her kisser. Bartholomew, get
              me my tools.

Bob Sergeant looks at the woman. Even under the blood
you can see she's top, top, top drawer.

                   BOB SERGEANT (CONT'D)
              I got me a Goddamn face to save.

CUT TO:

INT. SURGERY THEATRE. TWO DAYS LATER.

The Orderlies are knackered. Bob Sergeant is covered
in blood but his hair still looks good. The woman
is back to her very best, she looks at herself in a
mirror....

                         WOMAN
              But how...?

                      BOB SERGEANT
              Just doing my job 'Mam.

Bob Sergeant has one earring. A ruby. A gift from an
admirer (who else?!)

                   BOB SERGEANT (CONT'D)
              OK, boys. Go grab some shuteye.

The Orderlies leave. The woman turns to Bob Sergeant.

                         WOMAN
              Would you consider making love to
              me?

                      BOB SERGEANT
              Your stitches aren't set, sweet
              cheeks. If we made love then, no
              joke, your face would fall off.

                         WOMAN
              That would, and I genuinely mean
              this, be a small price to pay.

Bob Sergeant, against his better judgement, presses a
button and ALL HIS CLOTHES FALL OFF.

He MAKES LOVE TO THE WOMAN.

And, lo and behold, her face falls off.

                     WOMAN (CONT'D)
              How does it look?

                          BOB
              Appalling.

                    WOMAN
            Well, I had a ball.

Bob frowns and puts down his cocktail.

                 BOB SERGEANT
        Listen, there is one thing I could do.

        Bob picks up a mirror.

             BOB SERGEANT (CONT'D)
        Bartholomew, get me my tools.

                                            CUT TO:

INT. THEATRE. AN HOUR LATER.

                     BOB
            Well, what do you think?

                    WOMAN
            I've never been so happy.

REVEAL that Bob has made the woman a new face that is
an EXACT REPLICA OF BOB'S FACE.

                WOMAN (CONT'D)
        Would you consider making love to me?

                     BOB
            Well, I can hardly say I don't
            think you're a looker!

Bob and the Woman LAUGH LIKE DRAINS.

Bob presses a button and ALL HIS CLOTHES FALL OFF.

                                          CLOSE UP:

On Bartholomew. He smiles, rueful as Hell.

          BARTHOLOMEW THE GERMAN SHEPHERD
            'Ere we go'.

THE END

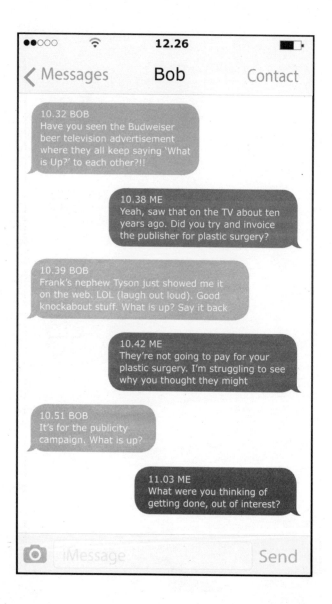

●●○○○ 🛜 **12.26** ▮▮▮▯

‹ Messages   Bob   Contact

10.32 BOB
Have you seen the Budweiser
beer television advertisement
where they all keep saying 'What
is Up?' to each other?!!

10.38 ME
Yeah, saw that on the TV about ten
years ago. Did you try and invoice
the publisher for plastic surgery?

10.39 BOB
Frank's nephew Tyson just showed me it
on the web. LOL (laugh out loud). Good
knockabout stuff. What is up? Say it back

10.42 ME
They're not going to pay for your
plastic surgery. I'm struggling to see
why you thought they might

10.51 BOB
It's for the publicity
campaign. What is up?

11.03 ME
What were you thinking of
getting done, out of interest?

📷 iMessage   Send

Business

Dear Bob,

I'm sick of being skint. As a successful businessman can you tell me how to earn the big bucks?

'Empty Pockets', Burnley

I'll never forget my friend Tommy telling me an intriguing theory about money. He explained that money is an energy. If you want to have it, then simply close your eyes and 'invite' that energy to come into your life. I found that fascinating. Tommy lost his house a few weeks later.

———————

Bob,

As a Scotsman recently moved to London to work in the creative industries, I've been absolutely flummoxed by the way people greet each other at lunches and work drinks. Single kiss, double kiss, hugs. What are the rules? It's like the Wild West. I met someone the other day and I was all over the place, I pretty much ended up putting her in a headlock. Help.

Paul I, Ealing

This sounds horrific and you have my full sympathies. I suggest you and your creative pals adopt the Dundee rules, which are very clear. Handshakes (no eye contact) for men, thumbs ups for women.

Bob,

Some career advice, please. I'm trying to decide between applying for the police and the army. The police seem to spend most of their time on mountain bikes these days while, according to their TV advert, being in the army is mostly windsurfing. Thoughts?

Flea, St Ives

These days the army spend the vast majority of their time recording charity songs and posing without their jumpers on for various causes. At worst, you'll probably have to learn a few knots and play a couple of games of cuckoo's nest in the buff. Having said that, the police is an absolute doddle. Gone are the days of chasing kids through apple orchards, and playfully clipping old women round the ear at bus stops. These days the police stroll about like they're in the FBI and all they want to do is get on *Crimewatch* and give 'shout outs' to their pals. It's 50/50, just toss a coin.

Hi Bob,

I'm trying to get promoted at work, but how do I go about it? Have you ever officially promoted Frank on the van? I'm a lawyer but I'm pretty sure the same rules apply.

Mark Y, Belsize Park, London

Frank has had a meteoric rise on the van. Like any apprentice he started on the napkins, but after just nine years, was handed a shock promotion to Deputy Manager (Onions). Just 12 years later, he was handed his dream job, Director of Sauces, the so-called 'floating role' of the cheeseburger-van trade. Fast-forward to today and Frank is nearing the end of his apprenticeship and will enter a five-year appraisal to see if he is ready to earn bumper, 'full time' wage. Yes, he's been lucky but he's worked for it and he deserves the riches that might one day arrive. I trust his story will prove an inspiration to you.[10]

―――――――――

Bob,

In tribute to your good self I'm thinking of starting a burger van. Would you consider sharing your 'recipe for success'?

Jimmy W, Leeds

I enclose my award-winning guide. Please send £5.99 by return of post.

―――――――――

10   I once worked out on a beer mat Frank's average hourly wage over the last 30 years. It was a spontaneous decision that I had extended cause to regret, standing in the rain later that evening watching him being talked down from the roof by the fire brigade.

"Minced Meat
Making Burgers tl

MEAT

If you're serious about running a burger van then you need a lot of meat. We buy a heavy bin bag of meat every morning from a fun-loving butcher in Carnoustie. We use a "collage" of meat, which is pretty much as good as it gets. Because our meat comes from a vast variety of animals, the healthy animals should almost always outweigh the sick ones. Which in turn gives our clients the best chance of having a healthy snack and not ending up in Sore Tummy Hell. It's a win-win-win.

BUNS

"Come and have some fun in a bun!" is our famous battle cry and it brings the punters sprinting from their little punter houses with their mouths hanging open like lizards. The great thing about serving buns is the vast opportunities for double, if not

triple, entendres. It's no coincidence that our van attracts an alarming number of divorcees, eager for some near-the-knuckle bawdy fun (in a bun).

LETTUCE

Introduced by the eighties "Yuppie" movement as part of their "Loadsamoney" culture was the idea of having bits of lettuce with cheeseburgers. In 1987 I invented the One-Finger Lettuce Shredder (™). I have, almost literally, never looked back.

ONIONS

We serve "triple cooked" onions extremely hot as an onion "lava".

SAUCES

Frank is Director of Sauces. Not my problem.

NAPKINS

Two for adults, one for kids. Otherwise I will, and please believe me on this, make you wish that you'd never been born.

Bob,

I've got a new boss and he's a bit of an oddball. He makes us work late, sometimes past five(!), and the other day he gave me a filthy look when he saw I was spending my morning perusing Wikipedia serial-killer entries. I'm too scared to even mention 'Thursday afternoon sardines', which me and a couple of the IT guys play if we've had a few pints at lunchtime. The job is glorified data entry, Bob, but this guy thinks he's running the Pentagon. How do we get him to ease off?

Ally R, Wapping, London

He needs to go and he needs to go now. The quickest (and fairest) way to get rid of him is for you to say the following: he invited you out for a chat on the fire escape. When you got there he produced his flaccid penis, upon which he had drawn a fairly accurate portrait of your face, and said, 'Shall we see what you look like with a big nose?' You were understandably all shook up but you'll let it go as long as the boy gets his jotters. Hope that helps. I can't see how it wouldn't.[11]

Alright Bob,

A business question. I'm the owner of a pub and we need a new fridge. As someone who spends all day in a hot van full of raw meat, I'm sure you have something pretty swish. What fridge have you got on the van?

Toby D, 'The Cuckoo's Nest', Tollcross, Edinburgh

We don't have a fridge.

----

11   I once witnessed Bob unsuccessfully use a version of this in an attempt to extricate himself from a punishing mobile-phone contract.

Bob,

I'd like to ask a top class businessman what the story is with VAT, as I've never really understood it. But I don't have contact details for a top-class businessman so can you help me instead?

'VAT's it all about?', Dumbarton

Firstly, grow up. Secondly, VAT is the best tax around. I call it the Very Awesome Tax because it's really up to you if you pay it or not. In fact, if I'm to be brutally honest with you I have never ███████ ███████████████████████████ cheese slices and lettuces ███████ ████████████████████ just said I grew them myself ███████ ██████████████████████ one for them and one for me ███████ ████████████████████████████ evasion not avoidance ███████ ████████████████████████████████ or maybe it's avoidance not evasion ████████████████████████ bin bag full of fivers ████████████████████████████████ literally down the back of the couch █████████████████████████████████████ Carol Vorderman █████████████████████████████████████ hardly the Crime of the Century ████████████████████████ ███████ go and catch the real criminals ████████████████ ███████ I can look myself in the mirror at night ███████ and greatly enjoy doing so ███████████████ quite frankly ███ ████████████████ they can go ███████ themselves.[12]

_____

Dear Bob,

It must be great to be on the BBC gravy train.

Pete S, Fulham, London

There's not as much gravy as you'd think.

---

12   For fairly obvious reasons I have edited this somewhat foolhardy response from Bob.

BBC Scotland

FAO Bob Servant
Bob Servant Enterprises,
Harbour View Road,
Broughty Ferry

Re: Expenses

Bob,

I'm writing to you with regards to the expenses claims for the recent filming of *Bob Servant* at your house in Broughty Ferry, Dundee. I'm afraid we have had to turn down the expenses claims listed below,

Best wishes,

Owen Bell

Producer, *Bob Servant*.

Rejected Claims

£75.42 for 50 packets of Space Invader crisps that you said were for 'local orphans' but we saw you eating on regular occasions.

£19.99 for a loudhailer that you used to 'contact' the director on set until it was confiscated.

£8.92 for the purchase of two pornographic magazines that you suggest helped you 'relax' during the 'stressful' filming period.

£27.54 for three bottles of Allure aftershave. We did not see any merit, or indeed logic, in your claim that 'A nice smell keeps everyone well.'

£50.00 for a director's chair with your name on the back (again, later confiscated).

£48.99 for ten hand-buzzers from a local joke shop which you described as 'critical morale tools'.

£89.99 for the ghetto blaster through which you played your 'walk on' music when you arrived at the set, including when you returned to the set from the toilet in the middle of a take (later confiscated).

£42.00 for a full body spray tan for you and a facial spray tan for your friend Frank, accompanied by a claim for £9.99 for a 'pair of skin colour gloves' in order for your friend Frank to 'stop his whining'.

£149.99 for the ten-man tent you erected on the edge of the set for a 'no pressure lunchtime mixer' between yourself and the cast and crew. Cast and crew reported that after being tricked into attending, your friend Frank zipped up the tent and you forcefully attempted to persuade them to support a coup d'état that would have replaced the director with yourself.

£240.00. This cost is a result of us discovering you had 'hired' two extras to do an additional day on set where their main job appeared to be to circulate around the crew spreading flattering rumours about yourself.

£432.17 for three hours in Smoky Joe's Recording Studio in Dundee. You claimed you were recording 'the theme tune'. We had never suggested you would be involved with the theme tune and when, under duress, you allowed us access to the studio recording, it solely featured you performing obscene versions of big-band classics.

On the last day of filming, a light aircraft towed a banner above the set that made a libellous claim about the director. You said at the time you were 'just as angry as he was' and would 'get to the bottom of who did this if it's the last thing I do'. You then submitted a receipt for £2,000, which, on closer inspection was for an aerial-advertising package and the creation of the aforementioned banner.

Bob,

I have to give an annual assessment to a co-worker. He's spent most of the year looking at dating websites and playing an online game that involves wizards. He's a good laugh though. So how does that balance out?

Dominic M, Connecticut, USA

The guy sounds like a keeper and if anything he should be promoted. Please disregard this advice if he's your co-pilot.

Bob,

Does your business do much for charity?

'Bob Aficionado', Hexham

Yes. In the old days if I made a joke at the van I'd double check that everyone who could hear the joke was making a purchase. But then I watched *Oliver Twist*. Seeing that horrible man fill little Oliver's pants with porridge, burning his fledgling genitals to a crisp,[13] shook me to the core. People need help. These days, my jokes are for everyone. It's the least I can do.

Bob,

I love a deal me. What's the best deal you've ever done?

'Wheeler Dealer', Solihull

---

13   Bob is dangerously misremembering the *Oliver Twist* plot here. Although Mark Lester, who played young Twist with such aplomb, faced enormous challenges in the role they fortunately did not include any such attack.

Two-thousand shop-soiled garden gnomes, £100 cash. I sold them round nursing homes at dusk and said they were angels. Easy money, apart from a couple of pathetic attempts to tie me to some early morning heart attacks.

Hi Bob,

A bit of your hard-earned advice, please. My daughter left school last year and is still looking for work. I know you're in the cheeseburger-van business–would that be a suitable trade for a young lady?

Roddy B, Paisley

Roddy, it literally pains me to say that a burger van is no place for a young woman. The amount of inappropriate attention I get as I go about my business is horrific. I am leered at several times a day, with everyone from traffic wardens to opportunistic members of the clergy subjecting me to their 'elevator eyes' as I serve them their burgers. They see me as a piece of meat, which is laced with cruel irony as I'm usually working with pieces of meat at the time. According to Frank's records, around 20 per cent of our customers are visibly aroused when ordering. And that can creep towards 25 per cent if I'm in my shorts. Every day's a struggle, Roddy, it's no place for a woman.

Dear Bob,

I'm applying for jobs and I get very nervous in interviews. Any advice?

'Dry Mouthed', Cardiff

I strongly advise you to listen to my relaxation tape and let your worries melt away like a snowman in a sauna. Please send £9.99 by return of post.[14]

---

14   I found and transcribed this tape. The cover art was not done by a professional.

Transcription Starts

Reggae music plays softly in background.

Bob: Let me take you on a journey. You're lying on a Caribbean beach covered in yellow sand. You've rubbed expensive suntan lotion over every inch of your body apart from your eyes.

Frank: And your undercarriage.

Bob: I'm doing the talking Frank.

Frank: Sorry.

Bob: All around you people laugh and drink Lilt straight out of the bottle. A frogman emerges from the water with a harpoon. He's caught an octopus, a dolphin and some smoked mackerel.

Frank: Not a bad day's work.

Bob: If you speak again, you'll wait in the van.

Frank: Sorry, Bob, I got sucked into the story.

(Sound of a deep breath)

Bob: You look out to sea. A fun-loving woman on water-skis is dragged through the waves. She shouts (voice becomes high-pitched) 'I'm having the most wonderful time!'

Frank: Can't blame her. Oh Christ. Sorry, Bob.

1

(Sound of a deep breath)

Bob: Up in a palm tree is a very pretty seagull. It flies down and lands on your left breast. And the seagull says, 'Alright mate? Just relax, have fun and take it easy. Just take it easy, real easy.' Listen to the seagull. Listen to the seagull, (voice becomes faint) listen to the seagull…

(Tape continues)

Bob: Did you see Cash in the Attic today?

Frank: The roller skates?

Bob: How did they think they were going to get any money for roller skates?

Frank: God knows.

Bob: They're in la la land.

Frank: I think the tape's still running, Bob.

Bob: Oh for Christ's sake.

RECORDING ENDS.

Dear Bob,

Just reading about the folk who made millions from inventing the loom band. Ever invented anything?

Gavin R, New York

I invented the phrase 'misters before sisters' in a bus stop in Carnoustie in 1963.

Dear Bob,

Looking to nail the smart-but-casual look at work this year. Comfortable with the clothes angle, need help on accompanying facial expressions. I was wondering about going for 'lusty rage'?

Ross T, Woking

Lusty rage is fine, but for legal reasons you should limit its usage to the sports field and newsagents (NOT supermarkets. CCTV only picks up half the story).

Hi Bob,

I've got to buy a new car. As a top-drawer businessman, can you school me in the art of negotiation?

Tommy S, Monifieth

Find enclosed my guide to negotiation. Please send £4.99 by return of post.

"NEVER GIVE AN INCH"

Bob Servant's Five Point Guide to Successful Negotiation

1. Get to the meeting early and put up topless photos of yourself doing sporty stuff.

2. When he or she comes in, let them 'accidentally' catch you doing press ups.

3. When they make their opening offer, laugh for a minimum of three minutes.

4. Take a call from a man from the United Arab Emirates who is offering to "blow the bidding out the water". I once did this to great effect while selling a barely used pair of long johns to an impressionable milkman. We were sparring away at the £3 mark but when I took the call from the "Sheikh" I had the milkman in my pocket and we closed the deal at a cool £4.25.

5. Do not cry during a negotiation.

Dear Bob,

While telling a light-hearted anecdote about my weekend at our Monday meeting this week, I unfortunately fell off my chair. Ever since then my colleagues have been giving me very little respect, which is a bit of an issue seeing as I'm the boss. How do I get them to take me seriously again?

Jake T, Swindon

The best way for anyone to increase their respect levels at work is to suggest that they are the perpetrators of violent crime. In the morning, let colleagues 'surprise' you washing blood from your hands in the toilet and explain things 'really kicked off' on the way to work. In the afternoon, go to the toilet and gouge deep scratches into your face, then return to your desk and say you've just 'whacked' someone in IT who was 'shit talking my baby mama'. The whole chair incident, and I can guarantee this, will soon be the least of your worries.

Bob,

A question from Texas. I got bad sunburn on the golf course yesterday. I'm supposed to have a big client meeting later to try and secure a sale for the company and I look idiotic. How's he going to trust me with his money when I can't be trusted to apply sun lotion?

'Red All Over', Houston

An easy one. Send an 'SMS' (mobile telephone text message) to the client explaining you're looking forward to meeting him but, as a word of warning, you get hopelessly embarrassed when in the company of handsome men. When you meet him immediately announce, 'Well, looks like it's a beamer for me, because you are hunky, hunky, hunky.' To make your position more convincing, hide a bottle of Lynx down your trousers to appear aroused and say, 'I think you'd better tell your doctor to stop giving you the handsome pills because someone is heading for an overdose!' then laugh and cover your mouth and say, 'Ooh, I just can't stop.' He'll be hopelessly flattered and the sale should go through more or less smoothly from there.

Hello Bob!

There's a park opened round the corner that they charge kids to get into. What kind of business is that? The centrepiece is a 'reflection pond' which currently has a lovely collection of kebab boxes floating in it. Ever thought of getting into the private-park game, Bob, and what would be in it?

'Park Life', Manchester

Bit of a sore one, this. In the late nineties, Dundee City Council announced they were going to redevelop Dawson Park which is, arguably, the Taj Mahal of Broughty Ferry. I submitted my plan and never heard a peep.

"A Park for the Punters"

Bob Servant's Dawson Masterplan

A LOVER'S LANE

Every park should have a lover's lane where fun-loving
couples can go to explore each other's bodies and whisper
the most extraordinary filth. To add to the mood, I will paint
slogans on a wall such as 'Sauce is Poss!(ible)', 'Everything
is Sauceible (i.e. possible)', and, for variety, 'There is a Real
Saucibility 'i.e. possibility' of Some Fun TONIGHT!'

AREA FOR MEN WHO CLASP THEIR HANDS BEHIND THEIR BACKS WHILE WALKING

Probably my greatest bugbear is men who clasp their hands
behind their backs while walking. They think they're army
generals inspecting their troops, but half the time they're
walking through the Safeways car park with soup all down
their fronts. So let's call their bluff. This will be the only area
of the park they're allowed to do it, and it will be next to the
bins. If they're proper claspers, they'll stay in that area and
deal with it. If not their clasping days are over, and not a
moment too soon.

PICNIC AREA

This is essentially a trap. I have the concession for all food
eaten at the park. So I will walk through the picnic area
kicking food out of people's hands, and quite rightly so.

'ROUNDABOUT INSANITY'

MONKEY BARS

No professionals.

JOKE AREA

This is essentially a trap. I have the concession for all jokes to be made at the park. I will walk through the area shouting over any illegal jokes, and quite rightly so.

BOB'S FLOWERY FACE

A large flower design of my face and hand, with a big beaming smile and the hand doing a mechanical 'thumbs up' that rocks back and forth and beckons the punters into the park. If anyone is caught tampering with this thumb to make it look like I'm masturbating, they will receive a lifetime ban from the park.

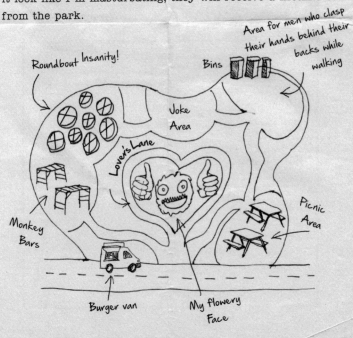

Roundbout Insanity!

Bins

Area for men who clasp their hands behind their backs while walking

Joke Area

Lover's Lane

Monkey Bars

Picnic Area

Burger van

My flowery Face

Right. Well that's obviously not going to happen

22.04 BOB
Pedalo Taxi Service

22.13 ME
Not sure what to say to that. Other than, obviously, no

22.43 BOB
Sports Personality of the Year?

22.57 ME
Can't see it. Unless you break a world record in your pedalo

23.01 BOB
I'll get back to you

23.15 ME
Don't feel you have to

Life Lessons

Dear Bob,

I got caught speeding, just a few MPH over, and my wife's carrying on like we're Bonnie and Clyde. What's a little soft crime between friends? I can't imagine you've always stayed strictly on the right side of the law. Should a crime be held against someone forever?

'Guilty Plea', Wigan

Absolutely not! People should be allowed to move on with their lives, because who knows what really happened? I have a rather chequered legal history, despite the efforts of my lawyer Objection McNally,[15] due to being targeted by rookie police officers who are keen to make a name for themselves. Through it all, I have maintained my dignity.

---

15 See *Dundee Yellow* Pages, p. 56: Objection McNally Lawyer Services – 'Don't Tell Me You Did It!'

Dundee Police Department
Incident Report #9005127
Report Entered: 07/08/2009   13:21:34

Incident Type/Offence

1.) ASSAULT
2.) DISORDERLY CONDUCT

Interviewing Officer
PC Paul Hegarty

Offender

Status	Name	Sex	Age	Phone	Address
DEFENDANT	Servant, Bob	Male			

Interview Narrative

PC Hegarty: Mr Servant, do you know why you're here today?

Bob Servant: Because my parents had sexual intercourse to the point of ejaculation. As was their right.

PC Hegarty: Mr Servant, do you know why you're at the police station today?

Bob Servant: I would like to plead the fifth.

PC Hegarty: That means nothing.

Bob Servant: Then I would like to invoke primae noctis.

PC Hegarty: If possible, that means even less.

Bob Servant: No comment.

PC Hegarty: I didn't ask you a question.

Bob Servant: Is that a two-way mirror?

PC Hegarty: That's not even a one-way mirror. It's just a wall.

Bob Servant: Whatever.

1

PC Hegarty: Mr Servant, can we talk about what happened this afternoon in Marks & Spencer?

Bob Servant: I went to buy some new threads and was the victim of a cruel joke by the shop attendant who swapped all the labels over on the clothes. The labels said 'Large' but the clothes were clearly 'Small'. I nearly dislocated my shoulder trying to get the cardigan on.

PC Hegarty: The attendant says he explained the clothes were correctly labelled and perhaps you required a larger size, and at that point you assaulted him.

Bob Servant: Nonsense.

PC Hegarty: You shouted, 'Let's see how you like it', and attempted to force a child's dress over the attendant's head.

Bob Servant: I made my point.

PC Hegarty: Mr Servant, can you give me a reason why we shouldn't charge you today with breach of the peace?

Bob Servant: I suppose it all comes back to the fable about the two horses.[16]

16   At this point, Bob told a forty-three minute fable about two horses who go on an epic adventure, where they meet a 'wizard with a goatee beard' who tells them various contradictory philosophies. With no warning, the story then relocates to the Arctic Circle, where the horses meet an 'Eskimo with a heart of gold' who tells them a lengthy anecdote about the importance of honesty amongst department-store workers. From listening to the tape, it sounds like PC Hegarty leaves the room at this point to get a sandwich, though Bob continues talking. When PC Hegarty returns the horses have taken on the not inconsiderable swim from the Arctic Circle to Australia where they have run into 'the one and only Mr Marks and Mr Spencer' in a 'gritty karaoke joint'. At this stage PC Hegarty ends the interview 'in the interests of my sanity' and gives Bob an on-the-spot fine of £25, which Bob claims as a 'moral victory'.

Bob,

What's the one thing a man needs in life more than any other?

Allan R, Edinburgh

I'd have to bow to my friend Tommy on this one. He's always said life can take everything from him, but as long as he has his 'peace of mind' then he'll be as right as rain. Although, now he's at the hostel, Tommy's also in the market for a personal safe.

Bob,

I'm a married father of two. I have a good job, am relatively fit for my age, always stand my round, and feel I still have a lot to offer. However, I've recently noticed I receive very little respect from my family. Have I made the wrong decisions in life to get to this worrying point?

'Where's the Respect?', Walthamstow, London

The quickest way for a man to gain respect in any situation is to employ a side parting. Simply apply the parting, take your seat at breakfast and let the parting get to work. Your wife and children will soon be eating out of your hands (literally, if that's a route you feel you want to go down).

Dear Bob,

Do ice-cream shops sell sundaes on a Saturday?

Jim S, via Twitter

Yes.

Dear Bob,

Mulling over a move to Australia. Thoughts?

Neal D, Dundee

I think you should go for it, pal. I've nothing but respect for those who try their luck in the colonies. I've often thought of selling up and heading to America's Deep South to work as a soul singer in a rough roadside bar. I'd live in a wee motel where the sign blinked on and off and have a torrid affair with the owner's wife, as long as their marriage was already in trouble and I wasn't the one breaking it up. And then I'd just come home. Good luck.

———————

Bob,

I've always wanted to be famous because it looks like a good laugh, with loads of dough and skirt on tap. As a telly star, Bob, can you tell me if it's all it's cracked up to be? Is fame worth it, Bob, or are there more important things in life?

'The Price of Fame', Dorset

Yes, the television documentary sent me into the big leagues, but I hardly came out unscathed. What they did to me was frankly outrageous, and when I was good enough to try to help they ignored me. Fame costs, there's no doubt about that one.

Enquiries at the burger van or in person at Stewpot's Bar, Broughty Ferry, after 6pm.
Not Bank Holidays (brings out the nutters).

Dear BBC Halfwits,

I have just watched the first episode of your documentary on me. Please find enclosed my edit notes. I expect every single one to be acted on with some haste.

1 min: What happened to my theme tune?

3 mins: That is not my body shape. You have used CGI to exaggerate certain areas in order to get a cheap joke. Please show the reality.

5 mins: That is not my running style. I run with a long, elegant gait. You have clearly sped up the footage to give me a more comical, 'scarpering' style. Amend.

6 mins: Actress looked unimpressed when I flirted with her. Do we have another take? Or can you Photoshop in another actress who is capable of giving a more believable reaction?

7 mins: Due to the weakness of the rest of the cast, my joke didn't quite 'land' there. Can you use special effects to make the other actors laugh and shake their heads as if to say, 'Here he goes again'?

8 mins: Eh? Makes no sense.

10 mins: Could you give just the slightest suggestion that I'm sexually aroused in this scene? Just add a telltale 'bump' to the corduroys. Not when I'm holding the cat though.

P.T.O.

12 mins: Too much talking from other actors. Boring.

14 mins: Get the camera on me please.

16 mins: I'm the shortest actor in this scene, which sends the wrong message. Please shorten the others by a foot each.

19 mins: That is not my smile. Change it.

21 mins: Eh? Makes no sense.

23 mins: You've butchered that joke. Absolutely butchered it.

25 mins: What the hell have you done to my hair? It looks like lady hair. Do you have any idea how that's going to play in Broughty Ferry? You're killing me.

27 mins: That's how I walk now is it? GET REAL.

29 mins: Oh here we go. Everyone laughs at Bob do they? You people are FUCKING IDIOTS.

30 mins: What happened to my theme tune?

Yours sincerely,

Bob

BBC Scotland

FAO Bob Servant
Bob Servant Enterprises,
Harbour View Road,
Broughty Ferry

Dear Bob,

Many thanks for sending over your intriguing 'edit notes'. As the episode you watched was in fact being broadcast on television, it would be slightly impractical and, indeed, pointless to go back and edit it now.

On another matter, we received a package from Broughty Ferry addressed to Neil Forsyth that had to be removed by Environmental Health. I couldn't help noticing the handwriting was similar to your own. The receipt of any future packages of that nature will force us to contact the police.

Best wishes,

Owen Bell

Producer, *Bob Servant.*

Bob,

My son has recently started Sunday school, which made me wonder, are you a religious man, Bob? Is there a parable from the 'good book' that you use to guide yourself through life's choppy waters?

'The Father, the Son, and the Holy Bob?', Dunfermline

I'm not a member of the God mob but I love a good read and the Bible has got the lot, mystery, erotica and some good knockabout humour. Probably my favourite parable is the one about Jesus going round to his pal's house. Jesus said to his pal, 'I'm going to nip over later, will you let me in?' and the boy said, 'Of course I will, Jesus, I'll stick a few cans of Kestrel in the fridge.'

Five minutes later there's a knock at the guy's door. It's a wee boy with sunglasses and he says, 'Can I come in Mister?' and the guy says, 'No chance, hop it.' Five minutes later, another knock at the door. It's an old woman wearing a baseball cap with 'BOYS, BOYS, BOYS' written on it. 'Ooh hello, room for a small one?' she asks. The guy says, 'I'm flattered, but no.' Five minutes later, another knock at the door. It's the boxer and heartthrob Frank Bruno. 'Hullo,' says Bruno. 'May I use your lavatory?' 'Sorry, Frank,' says the guy, 'Never been a fan. It ain't going to happen.'

Five minutes later, a knock at the door. It's Jesus. 'Thank God, no pun intended,' says Jesus's friend. 'It's been a strange old day. In you come.' But Jesus says, 'I would rather defecate in my pants than come into your house. I have appeared to you three times. As a wee boy with sunglasses, as an old woman with a baseball cap with "BOYS, BOYS, BOYS" written on it, and as the boxer and heartthrob Frank Bruno, and each time you have turned me away.' And then Jesus went and got the bus home.

Hi Bob,

What's been your biggest disappointment in life?

Carol H, Epsom

My off-peak timeshare at the 'Adults Only' static caravan park in Pitlochry. The brochure made it sound like the Last Days of Rome. In 18 years I've seen three women there, and two were with the Fire Brigade after the boy at number 18 cracked and did a ham-fisted insurance job. Can't blame him. My caravan's got subsidence, going to bed is like scaling the north face of Kilimanjaro.

Bob,

If I could only ask you one question it would be this–what's the story with wearing sunglasses inside? Who's allowed to do it?

Alex V K, London

Only the blind and the famous. The same goes for running your hands across the faces of strangers when you meet them.

Dear Bob,

I live (God help me) in Cumbernauld. I like the odd pint but the pubs are bussing in bouncers from Glasgow. They're a scary bunch and I'm only a wee guy. How can I get over my fear and get back in the boozers where I belong? I think if I can crack this one my whole life will change for the better.

Wee Davie McD, Cumbernauld

The key with bouncers is to unsettle them by giving them a saucy, 'anything's possible' look, similar to those you used to get in the Carry On films and from fellow passengers in the early days of Intercity trains. That should work out just about fine.

Bob,

What's the one thing you wish you'd done but have failed miserably to do?

Alan F, Fulham, London

While it's not been a failure on my part, as I did everything I could, I suppose it would be 'The Bob Sergeant Adventures' not making it on to the telly. Really, that's a failure for mankind as a whole.

THE BOB SERGEANT ADVENTURES
Episode 4 — "THE LAST WITHDRAWAL"

FADE IN:

INT. OFFICE.

Bob Sergeant the Sexy Bank Manager of Broughty Ferry sits in his office thinking to himself, "Bobby 'ole (old) boy, you got it made."

And he has. The office is top, top, top level. His chair is made of leather that is as smooth as butter. His buttocks just sink right in there. It's genuinely as if he's sitting on butter. Pure luxury.

On his desk he's got one of those things with the metal balls that swing back and forth.

Bob's buttocks sink even deeper into the butter-like chair. They're getting right in there. Real deep. Bob Sergeant leans back in his chair and runs both hands all the way through his hair. His hair looks like liquid gold and runs all the way down to his thighs.

A WOMAN walks in dressed up to the nines.

> WOMAN
> I'd like a loan please. I need a
> whole lotta (lot of) money.

Bob Sergeant presses a button and ALL HIS CLOTHES FALL OFF.

> WOMAN (CONT'D)
> What on Earth are you doing?

Bob Sergeant puts his clothes back on.

> BOB SERGEANT
> Sorry love.

> WOMAN
> I'd love to hear your terms?

Bob Sergeant presses a button and ALL HIS CLOTHES
FALL OFF.

> WOMAN (CONT'D)
> What's wrong with you?

Bob Sergeant puts his clothes back on.

> BOB SERGEANT
> You're kind of sending me mixed
> signals here.

> WOMAN
> I'd like to apply for...

Bob Sergeant reaches for the button...

> WOMAN (CONT'D)
> Stop it. OK?

> BOB SERGEANT
> OK.

> WOMAN
> Promise?

> BOB
> I promise to try.

Silence.

> WOMAN
> Can you show me your interest
> rate?

Bob Sergeant presses a button and ALL HIS CLOTHES
FALL OFF.

THE END

Bob,

You've attracted a fair number of misguided critics over the years, great men always do of course. What's the worst thing anyone's ever said about you?

Peter and Judy E, Ockley

For 30 years I've been plagued by a woman from Fife who believes I stole her walk. The idea I'd steal a walk from anyone is absurd. The idea I'd steal it from a woman from Fife is the stuff of nightmares.

———————

Bob,

Money makes the world go round, that's what they say. Not the scientist mob, but you know what I mean. Is that really all that it's about Bob? There has to be more to life surely,

'Rich in Soul', Bournemouth

Of course there is and scientists will tell you that the boys who spend their time chasing the big bucks didn't do too well with the skirt when they were at school. The way I see it, as long as I can get up in the morning and look myself in the mirror and see that I'm wearing pyjamas made entirely out of stitched together large denomination banknotes, then I'm happy. Money simply doesn't come into it.

———————

Dear Bob,

As a fellow jumper fan, would you agree with me that a big part of life is making sure you have a really nice jumper?

Mike K, Shawlands, Glasgow

Absolutely. Good jumpers are like good dreams: you don't know where they come from and you want to tell your postie all about them. They say by the time he's 50 a man has the jumper he deserves. I hope for your sake it's a good one.

Hi Bob,

You're not getting any younger. As a lawyer I was wondering if you've written your will?

Derek S, Ayrshire

I have.

'He Left 'Em Wanting More'

The Last Will and Tenement
of Robert Servant

I leave my extension to the good people of Broughty Ferry. In return, the anniversary of my death will be known forever as 'Bob Fest'. Every man, woman and child will dress up as me in a bunnet and moustache. Out of respect, those outfits will remain on during any lovemaking. On 'Bob Fest', murals of me will be proudly displayed around Broughty Ferry. If anyone draws testicles dangling from my ears like testicle earrings or from my chin as a testicle beard then they will be sent to prison.

I leave my One-Finger Lettuce Shredder invention to my paperboy, Darren. He's ready.

I leave my collection of soft-core pornographic aprons to the Dundee Museum of Art for them to use in a major exhibition entitled 'All Down His Front ' The Life, Times and Aprons of Robert Servant'.

I leave my Andy Murray nickname, 'The Dunblane Hydro', to the nation.

I leave my joke of tapping people on one shoulder but then running round the other side to Frank's nephew Tyson. He's ready.

P.T.O.

I leave my trampoline collection to the Fire Brigade for use in rescue missions and not as toys.

I leave the following to my friend and right-hand-man Frank - the burger van and all fittings, the recipes for the finest burgers in the western hemisphere, permission to use all of my jokes to the best of his ability, my You've Been Framed back catalogue on VHS, the cardboard box under my stairs marked 'Don't Look And Even If You Do This Stuff Isn't Mine It Came With The House', my jumper and cardigan collection, the static caravan, £18.72 credit at Zapzone and the saying 'onions for show, burgers for dough'.

Dear Bob,

A few years ago I loaned you the deposit to stand for election as an independent candidate for our hometown of Broughty Ferry. The money had been saved to provide me with a new bathroom suite. History shows that the deposit was lost. Is there any chance whatsoever of me seeing the money again? As you are aware, I had already removed my previous bathroom. Living without a bathroom is an enormous challenge, hence my question to you today.

Yours in distress,

Frank, Broughty Ferry, Dundee

Frank, as I've told you many times, that deposit was a small price to pay for the important life lesson of 'don't be hasty'. With regards to your self-inflicted toilet situation, you live less than 300 metres from the bowling club and only have to climb over two walls to get there. If you fail to make that journey without incident then that is a nutritional issue for which I cannot be reasonably asked to take responsibility.

Hi Bob,

What's the correct term for someone you meet on holiday but don't like?

Max W, Singapore

A bellendio.

Bob,

As a fellow 'senior' member of society I wanted to ask what you think is the hardest thing about getting old?

'Old Codger', Carlisle

Probably the way my looks are maturing. I always hoped that my looks would mature badly, that in my later years I'd be able to shake off the skirt and concentrate on the bowling but I'm sad to say the reverse is happening. I'm aging superbly, the skirt is still being dragged along on my coattails (often literally) and my bowling remains highly unpredictable.

Dear Bob,

What has been your greatest embarrassment?

Joan F, Broughty Ferry

In 1983 I accidentally wore my jumper inside out to a bowling-club disco in Carnoustie. Sometimes I wonder if I ever recovered.

Bob,

Any regrets?

Simon T, San Pedro, Guatemala

Two. I wish I hadn't offered so much encouragement to Idi Amin but, to be fair to me, he was just a guy on a bus with a dream. My biggest regret is losing my only VHS copy of *Bus Conductresses Gone Wild* on the waltzers at Broughty Ferry Gala Week in 1987. It dropped into the machinery and was smashed to smithereens. To this day I wake up screaming at the memory.

Dear Bob,

What's it all about?

Stewart F, Broughty Ferry, Dundee

A fine question from a fine place. Stewart, the more life I live, the more I realise that it's all about your walk. My walk is essentially a jazz piece. There's no real structure to it and no two performances are exactly the same. I've picked up influences everywhere from movie stars to traditional marching bands to nature documentaries, and the result is astonishing. Get yourself a good walk, my friends, and you'll get yourselves a good life. Thanks for all of your questions, it's been a ball.

Your Servant,

Bob Servant

La comédie est terminée

Servant Retires (Again)

Broughty Ferry businessman Bob Servant has called time on the reprisal of his burger-van empire, saying he wants more time to 'dream big and watch the telly'. Servant originally hung up his apron in the wake of Dundee's Cheeseburger Wars in the eighties before making what he termed his 'Second Coming' last year.

'Frank Sinatra'

'The punters wanted us back and we delivered,' said Servant. 'Now it's time for me to take a step back and consider my next move.' 'People say that I've made more comebacks than Frank Sinatra,' joked Servant, who was unable to clarify who the aforementioned 'people' are. 'I'm not one to brag,' he added, 'but I'm a great guy.'

'Outer Space'

'When I look back on my life,' said Servant, 'I see some of the greatest glories imaginable. The longest window-cleaning round in western Europe and a burger-van collection that, at its peak, could be seen from outer space. More skirt than I, genuinely, have known what to do with, and thousands upon thousands of happy punters. The fact that I have managed to stay humble is perhaps my greatest achievement of all.'

Servant has denied his decision to close his burger van is connected to 18 outstanding Health and Safety writs, which he described as '18 storms in 18 teacups'.

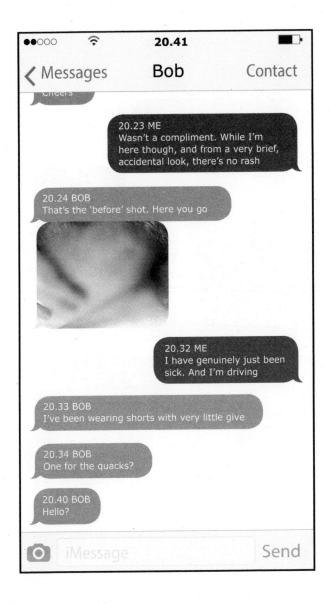

Acknowledgements

Thanks to Lorna Russell, Charlotte Macdonald, Claire Scott and all at Ebury/BBC Books who have been so supportive of Bob's efforts. Thanks, as ever, to David Riding and all at MBA. David has dealt with Bob for nearly ten years and I think the effects are starting to show. Thanks to Owen Bell, Ewan Angus and everyone at BBC Scotland for asking me to thrust Bob upon a bewildered nation. Thanks to Brian Cox and Jonathan Watson for being the best Bob and Frank imaginable.

Thanks to Lee Healey (who draws *Viz* magazine's superlative Drunken Bakers amongst others) for assisting Bob with his etchings in this book, thanks to Graham Gillies at BBC Scotland who helped Bob with his burger posters, and thanks to Marcus Scudamore for his brilliant design of the book.

A massive thanks to all of you who have spent years sending in *Ask Bob* requests for Bob's guidance. Some of you were on those first emails ten years ago, sent in Friday afternoon giddiness, when I introduced you to a Broughty Ferry cheeseburger kingpin called Bob Servant. And look what happened. Amazing. Thanks for being part of it.

A big 'Dundee hello' to Mum, Dad, Alan and Carol. And my thanks, love and (almost) limitless respect to my top, top, top-level wife Rhiannon, who has to read this stuff when it's in an even more primitive state, who barely reacts when she finds me making a sex toy in the kitchen out of a trowel, and who diligently spends a morning sticking slogans to the crotches of corduroy trousers.

And now, I suppose, to Bob. It was, as expected, a difficult time in Broughty Ferry pulling the book together. Long days in Bob's extension reading through his files with him sitting uncomfortably close, asking, 'Which bit are you laughing at?' when I wasn't laughing, and offering me an unnecessary handkerchief when he passed me 'a tearjerker'. And then comes the final day – which is always the hardest.

———————

I find Bob and his sidekick Frank in Broughty Ferry's Stewpot's Bar, the hostelry that Bob calls 'the pub of a thousand smiles'. He's annoyed with me. Yesterday Bob asked me to speak to the BBC about his Bob Sergeant creation. I'd told him that, as unpredictable as the BBC commissioning process can be, I was confident they wouldn't be interested in the adventures of a multi-profession sex maniac. He'd told me I was a 'Palestinian'. I asked if he meant 'Philistine' and he asked me to leave.

So it's a difficult atmosphere in Stewpot's Bar, one I attempt to lighten by congratulating Bob on another completed book. He softens a little, saying that seeing *Ask Bob* fully compiled, with all those notes from all those people, has made him feel funny. 'Not like God *exactly*...' he says.

'Shall we go for a walk?' I intervene.

Bob, Frank and I walk along Broughty Ferry's Brook Street, a road Bob refers to as 'The Walk of Fame'. It's difficult to concisely describe the experience of walking through Broughty Ferry in Bob's company. Perhaps it would be easier to summarise this particular journey:

Bob suffers three unreturned high fives in succession then declares he's not 'giving out' any more if people are 'too immature to accept them'.

Bob tells me an approaching woman is 'not so much an old flame, more of an old inferno'. Frank helpfully points out to me that an inferno is 'bigger' than a flame. The woman walks past us without any sign of recognition. Bob says she's obviously 'still hurting' and 'a prisoner of the past'.

An elderly member of the clergy sees Bob approach and jogs away.

Frank says he needs to sit down. Earlier that day he dropped a box full of frozen onion rings on his foot. 'Part frozen,' Bob corrects him.

Bob sees a man in a café and aggressively cajoles him out to the street. Bob points out how much the man resembles the television presenter Des Lynam (he doesn't) and firmly states it was him who first gave the man the 'lookalike'. The man angrily wrestles himself free from Bob and returns to his befuddled wife in the café. Bob, his palms raised in despair, tells me, 'This is what I'm up against'.

I mention that Broughty Ferry has a *joie de vivre*. Bob says it doesn't, but there's a Caffè Nero.

Bob makes us cross the road to avoid three women pushing infant children in prams. He calls them a 'hen party' and reveals his fear that they would try and 'touch me up'. Bob starts to speculate where on his body their attack would 'inevitably concentrate...'

'Shall we go down to the river?' I intervene.

———

Down at Broughty Ferry harbour, the three of us sit on Bob and Frank's favoured bench, looking out over the river Tay. Bob produces cans of beer from the folds of his jacket. There's a moment of charming unity – where Bob announces, 'We're like the Three Musketeers...' – which lasts until he adds, '...Dogtanian, Shorty and Bellend.' Although the names aren't individually assigned, I'm confident Bob's awarding himself Dogtanian, and Frank's a lot shorter than me.[17]

Tensions arise between Bob and Frank after Frank adopts a seating position on the bench with one leg lifted over the other. Bob accuses him of 'unspeakable arrogance' and 'sitting there like you're Michael Parkinson, or something'. Frank readjusts his position and apologises for being a 'cocky long legs'.

17   As he refers to D'Artagan, who wasn't one of the Musketeers, Bob's presumably working off the cartoon *Dogtanian and the Three Muskehounds,* which was a later work, oh, who gives a shit, it's nearly over...

I tentatively ask Bob about his future plans and he tells me that when life 'has my balls in a vice', he reacts by 'grabbing life by the balls'. Keen to avoid further examination of this testicular Mexican standoff and looking for an exit, I bring up this Acknowledgements section. It's the last work to be done on the book. I ask Bob if he'd like to include anyone, Frank perhaps. After all, Frank's his best friend.

'Top five,' clarifies Bob, edgily, and Frank looks as if he might explode with joy at the heady ranking.

Bob says he hopes more than anything that the book sends a message of 'friendship and solidarity' to 'the Brazilian favelas'. Bob talks about the favelas a lot, the result of his recently chancing upon a late-night documentary. I assure him that the Brazilian favelas will undoubtedly be the book's main market.

'I suppose,' continues Bob, clearing his throat, 'you could also say hello to Frank. If there's room.'

Frank gasps with pleasure. It's a charming moment and the three of us sink into contemplation. I find myself thinking about Bob. All the years we've spent connected, and now there is to be a farewell, of sorts. As time passes on the bench, I can tell from Bob's demeanour that he is thinking the same. How do we effectively capture what this moment might mean? As Dundonian men, we lack the tools for such emotional exchanges. I decide to help us both. I stand and say, simply but loaded with subtext, 'I'm going now.'

Bob turns to me. 'I'd genuinely forgotten,' he says, 'that you were here.'

I leave them on the bench and walk across the cobbled pier. Broughty Ferry catches the last of the evening sun, which dips into the river beyond the Tay Bridge. I look back just once as I reach the road. Bob and Frank haven't moved. They look out across the water in the fading light. Bob pats Frank once, lightly, on the head.

Neil Forsyth
West Sussex
August 2015

Index

★ **BEAU**...

Bob's

SERVING MINCEMEA...

BEAUTIFUL
Bob's Burgers

Open for Breakfast, Dinner and your Tea!

Also cater for Parties (Birthdays, Divorce, Funerals, Your Son's First Skirt etc)

FUL

Burgers

...10 DREAMS SINCE 1982

...TTENTION BELLENDS

Bellends will not be served. If you have previously been identified by Bob as being a Bellend then the ban can only be lifted if you bring a letter from your Doctor explaining why you were temporarily acting like a Bellend and guaranteeing that you are medically no longer a Bellend.

NUTRITIONAL INFORMATION

Fat 0%
Calories 0%
Poison 0%
'Mad Cow' 0%
Good Stuff 100%

TERMS AND CONDITIONS

Joke Policy. Customers are not permitted to make jokes or tell funny anecdotes within twenty yards of the van unless requested to do by Bob. All other jokes and anecdotes will be provided free of charge by Bob. Bob should not be expected to spend his days listening to jokes and stories told by amateurs. That's insane.

Refund Policy. Refund Requests to be made in person at Stewpot's Bar, Broughty Ferry between 11pm and midnight. Dress code is formal. Refund Request meetings begin with the national anthem, followed by 45 minutes of 'getting to know you' line dancing (we use a 'fusion' tape of Country and Western and Doo-Wop), followed by your presentation. Your chances of a Refund will be greatly improved if you do a funny impression or use 'dry ice'.

1 3 5 7 9 10 8 6 4 2

BBC Books, an imprint of Ebury Publishing
20 Vauxhall Bridge Road,
London SW1V 2SA

BBC Books is part of the Penguin Random House group of companies whose addresses
can be found at global.penguinrandomhouse.com

Penguin
Random House
UK

First published by BBC Books in 2015

www.eburypublishing.co.uk

A CIP catalogue record for this book is available from the British Library

ISBN 9781785940132

Commissioning Editor: Lorna Russell
Editor: Charlotte Macdonald
Design: Amazing15
Cartoons on pages 67, 69, 97, 182 © Lee Healey

Printed and bound in Great Britain by Clays Ltd, St Ives PLC

Penguin Random House is committed to a sustainable future for our business,
our readers and our planet. This book is made from Forest Stewardship Council®
certified paper.